Advance Acclaim for

Follow Your Bliss, Not Your Blisters

Nanci practices what she preaches and lives unconditionally happy. If you desire happiness to be your go-to response to life's challenges, please read this book.

Darrin Zeer, Best-selling author & America's Relaxation Expert

The way of "upliftment" is Nanci's way. As Nanci accomplished in hospitality, she now lays out the way for all of us.

Chip Conley, New York Times bestselling author and hospitality entrepreneur

The ideas in this book are memorable, humorous and yet profoundly and deceptively simple, which elevates it to the category of bona fide wisdom. Read it, Use it, apply it daily, re- read it, what is required to achieve happiness mastery is at your fingertips.... All you need to do is Follow Your Bliss Not Your Blisters.

Holly Stiel, Author, Speaker, President Thank You Very Much, Inc.

I have worked with Nanci in transforming businesses on three continents, and I've repeatedly seen her accomplish things others say is not possible. Simply put, she brings out abilities and qualities in people that they did not even know they had. In this book, Nanci shares the same processes and inspiration she achieved in hospitality with people everywhere. I recommend it highly.

Barry Pogorel, Crossroads Consulting Group

Happiness requires making good choices. Nanci lays out considerations for effective decision making. If your goal is to have a life you love, a life you control, I recommend Follow Your Bliss, Not Your Blisters as a must read.

Richard Wagman, PhD. Psychology

"No one is responsible for your happiness" — Everyone knows that but some still cling to the idea that something other than themselves can work that miracle. Whichever category you fall into, this book will either validate or teach you. Written in pithy easy to read language that captures the essence of Sherman's thesis, it's a carry-in-your-briefcase or read on whichever line you're standing book. You'll laugh and smile and nod your head and may even convert a nosy stranger curious to know what has captured you — into a friend. Or you might want to respond simply: "Happiness."

Emily Rosen, M.A., M.S. — Teacher, Editor, Mental health counselor, author.

Follow Your BLISS, Not Your BLISTERS

How to Live Unconditionally Happy

NANCI SHERMAN

www.followyourbliss.today
Cover Design by Shuma Malik
2018 Golden Retriever Publishing
ISBN

Disclaimer

This book is designed to provide information and motivation to our readers. It is sold with the understanding that the author is not engaged to render any type of psychological, legal, or any other kind of professional advice. The content of each article is the sole expression and opinion of the. No warranties or guarantees are expressed or implied by the publisher's choice to include any of the content in this volume. Neither the publisher nor the individual author shall be liable for any physical, psychological, emotional, financial, or commercial damages, including, but not limited to, special, incidental, consequential or other damages. Our views and rights are the same: You are responsible for your own choices, actions, and results.

Contact the author at

sherman.nanci@gmail.com for inquiries.

Dedication

To my mom Charlotte for her unshakeable joie de vivre, and to all my sisters and brothers out there, may you live "happy" ever after.

Table of "Content"edness

Self-Actualization: The Way Up

The Summer Day

"Doesn't everything die at last,
and too soon?

Tell me, what is it you plan to do
with your one wild and precious
life?"

— Mary Oliver

Introduction

Your special path

This book is about living unconditionally. Unconditionally happy. Unhindered. Free.

The distinctions I lay out for your consideration will have a direct impact on your ability to live a life you love and love the life you live.

First, allow me to introduce myself.

I am not one of the enlightened ones who left my body to come back and tell you how it all works out in the end. Guru is not on my business card. "Know thyself" is not a shingle I hang outside my door.

And yet… I am always happy.

But it wasn't always that way.

The happiness I speak of refers to a state of being, not a mercurial emotion. Even if I get pissed off at something, I get back to "happy" very quickly. It is a set point I learned to develop to navigate my time here.

Pondering this one afternoon. I asked myself, "How did I achieve this state of mind?" Certainly, I have had failures, letdowns, and unrequited love. These unplanned and unwanted events took me down a few notches, for sure. But I never lost sight of my True North – living joyfully. I realized that happiness, practiced as a way of life, is a benefactor I can count on.

And that's when I decided to write this book. It is about what I discovered and what I had to learn to let go of to achieve joy, day by day, regardless of pending circumstances. (Disclaimer: There will always be major life challenges that will throw us off track now and then. There are the clear life and death situations that shake our very being, but you will see that whatever else pushes our happiness switch to "off mode" may no longer be justifiable).

Everyone wants to feel on top of the world but all too often we struggle with the climb. We claim reasons and circumstances for why we fall short. "Maybe my inspiration is on an extended vacation," you say. But as you read on, you will discover that many of our justifications are not as insurmountable as you think.

Pogo put it best: "We have met the enemy and he is us."

What follows is a synthesis of what I have sought out, learned from masters of consciousness and awareness, and personally experienced. Over the years I acquired fresh insights on reconsidering my own obstacles to happiness. My hope is that you too will gain a newfound perspective and agility to break through whatever might be holding your happiness hostage. Let's look at those shackles for what they are and what they aren't.

This is your special path. I only wish to make a contribution.

Flexing Your Happiness Muscle

Where it is and what is it

If someone asked you to describe your day to day self in three adjectives, would one of the them be "happy?" If not, read on. There's a "happ" for that!

I will begin by giving credit where credit is due. Joseph Campbell was a prolific author and lecturer on the human spirit. His philosophy is summarized as "Follow Your Bliss."

"If you follow your bliss, you put yourself on a kind of track that has been there all the while, waiting for you, and the life that you ought to be living is the one you are living. Wherever you are — if you are following your bliss, you are enjoying that refreshment, that life within you, all the time."

Thank you, Joseph. We are about to dive in.

First, what happiness is not:

It is not a future based, somewhere over the rainbow, someday destination. It is not manic elation or a mercurial emotion responding willy-nilly to outside conditions. I don't believe in the pursuit of happiness, per se. Happiness isn't a goal. What interests me is how to be happy now, now, now!

In this book, I lay out a road map for your consideration so that "happy" for no reason and every reason becomes your predominant way of being – your default state. You won't avoid issues. You will feel happy despite them. Even when situations and people don't live up to your expectations, you won't succumb to struggle and angst mode. This book is about how to cultivate and nurture that.

It's not as if you will become immune to human emotions. You will still get sad, disappointed, and pissed off. Loved ones will pass on and dogs will too. The difference is that once you know how to flex your happiness muscle, you will be in more control of your life regardless of the winds that come along blowing you this way and that.

Specifically, the kind of happiness I refer to is the liberation you give yourself, free from obstacles, conditions, guilt, you name it. In other words, people and things don't have to be a certain way for you to feel good. That is also what I call freedom.

Start noticing where you spend your attention. Is it on what is wrong with you or them? What you think is missing or how "fair" life is. While we build our happiness muscle, we also increase our energy. Consider what drains your energy including situations and institutions that demand much from you. Do they add joy or feel like obligation? Empowerment is something we give to ourselves. No one can give it to you. And any one taking it from you is a thief.

Happy runs the gamut from feeling relief after having a splinter removed to satisfaction, joy and enthusiasm. In all stages of happy you *feel* good. That's how you know you are somewhere on the spectrum.

One thing to be clear about. Your happiness does not include stepping on other people or their shadows. I suggest that no one can be truly happy if they harm another in any way.

What I propose within these pages is easy to access – it doesn't require uninspired and excessive "efforting"- affirmations, gratitude journals, exercises, or meditation (although always recommended). Even if there is an event or a person that just won't live up to your expectations, we've got that covered too.

DISTINCTION:

Happiness is a gift you give yourself and others. To live joyfully is to feel love all around you even if you are the only one in the room.

Living Unconditionally Happy

Achieving Freedom

What does it mean to live unconditionally happy? It means you are happy for no reason or every reason. Conditions exist but don't thwart you. You feel a connectedness to all things regardless of what is happening around you. You feel plugged into universal energy. You sense that everything is working out for you no matter what is happening now. You live with a sense of great expectation of what's to come. All that matters in the present moment is you find something to feel good about. It could be anything that lights you up. A wonderful book. Cloud formations. A yummy sandwich. You will come to realize that your life is contingent upon what you think about and how to control that.

Imagine being the ocean. (Not so foreign. We are 80% water). As the ocean we are the environment and the one constant against which all matters of sea life play out. It is the same for us. Our minds are the environment in which all forms of emotion and thoughts take place. You will come to realize you are not your thoughts. You are the playground in which thoughts occur, but whether they stick around for an extended visit or not is your choice.

Feelings pass.

Opinions shift.

Conditions change.

With an awakened consciousness, thoughts ebb and flow like the tide.

Cultivating a Mastermind

How to design a happy brain

Your destiny is joy and freedom. However, all too often we experience obstacles to the full realization of that.

I don't know of anyone who is not seeking what will make them happy or at least happier.

Most of the processes in our body are regulated by the autonomic nervous system. We don't have to press a saliva button when presented with our favorite meal. Digestive juices just show up. Our brain is no different. Once we have laid down the initial "rules" of behavior for ourselves and others, the brain instructs us what our habitual reaction needs to be. The brain recalls the past and uses it to predict a future. You could say it arrests the unconscious mind by masquerading as free choice.

Our mind and brain report to each other but the brain thinks it's the big boss and the mind is the mere servant of the viewpoints it spawns. The brain isn't concerned with happiness. Its only concern is survival. In developing a Mastermind, we seek to flip the master/servant relationship, so the mind teaches the brain new ways to design our destiny.

You are familiar with the expression, "Make up your mind." There is nothing truer than the fact that you can make your mind up to be anything. Including being happy.

On Distinctions

Achieving clarity

This is a book about distinctions. Distinctions matter. A lot.

To create distinction in all matters of your life is to see more clearly. Clarity exposes us to things we haven't noticed before. Options and opportunities reveal themselves that otherwise would be beyond our ken. There is a whole world out there beyond what we currently perceive and once we do, "Shift" happens!

With a fresh and liberating perspective, you will choose what you want to have in your life and what you don't want in it. With that in mind, I have divided the book into three sections:

Undressing the Self: Revealing the Path to Personal Reality: A look at how we got to be who we are today.

Freedom: The Art of Letting Go: How to release futile and habitual responses to make way for happy and effective ones.

Self-Actualization: The Way Up: How to fulfill your highest potential.

Play with weights, you will build arm strength. Play with me, you will build your happiness muscle.

“Be in love with your life. Every moment of it.”

— Jack Kerouac

Undressing the Self: Revealing the Path to Personal Reality

How you got to be you

We aren't born as a turnkey operation - marinated, baked, and ready to go. To undress the self requires going back to when we were first born – a blank slate without imprint (as far as we know) and with unlimited potential. Immediately thereafter, we begin to bake into our psyche the sensory impressions and beliefs that make up who we are today.

We will explore how you became you. You will understand why you do what you do, why you have what you have, and why you think what you think. Only when we take the time to observe ourselves can we create a life by design, not default. We will fill our closet with what we want to dress ourselves in and discard what we have outgrown.

Decision making (all your choices) and living a life you love are inextricable. Follow Your Bliss, Not Your Blisters is a resource for you to reconsider whether past decisions you are still living with today and future ones are aligned with your life's purpose(s).

Your first courses of study at the University of Happy (aka Happy U) will be on Revealing our Programming and Effective Decision Making.

Believe It or Not!

Why we believe what we believe

This common expression powerfully sums up the totality of our psychological, spiritual, and physical make-up. What we come to believe about ourselves and others early in life becomes the foundation upon which everything else rests. It is an imprint. That is the nature of beliefs. They will continue to inform the psyche until one day, when things may not be working out as we had hoped, expected and planned, we are nudged to crack them open and see them for what they really are.

Systems of any kind are defined as independent elements working together to form a unified whole. So it is with our belief system. We will dissect how we created our individual world views, consider if they currently serve our noble purpose, and sort it out from there. A point of view is, in fact, a point of YOU.

We *Become* what we *Believe.* That is the nature of beliefs.

Instead of "To be or not to be," William Shakespeare could have had Hamlet say, "To believe, or not to believe." *That* is really the question.

Monk on the Mountain

The how and what of enlightenment

A woman struggles for years to become enlightened. She goes from teacher to guru to oracle to mentor. None of the prophets or avatars could answer her burning question, "What is the meaning of life?" One day, after struggling for a week to get to the top of a mountain to see whom many sages said was the "Most Enlightened One" the woman reached the summit to make her inquiry.

"Oh, Great One. What is the meaning of life?" the exhausted student asked.

The guru stroked his beard, gazed into the expectant eyes of the questioner and answered, "Why my lady, life is like a waterfall."

"A waterfall?" she echoed, a look of doubt in her eyes.

The Monk on the Mountain regarded the look on her face, and said, "You mean it isn't?"

DISTINCTION:

One person's belief is another person's "huh?" Our ideologies form early in life. We innocently accept the imprints. As our belief structures take hold, it is often to the exclusion of exposure to alternate opinions. What I am about to suggest will and should shake your foundation.

Even though we treat our beliefs as true, they are in fact, firmly held opinions. Opinions are not necessarily based on facts and beliefs are not necessarily based on proof… and both are subject to change. The most important and relevant inquiry about your beliefs should be "Does this belief serve me or is it a block to my sense of well-being?"

We will begin undressing ourselves by examining the three biggies that are responsible for our current beliefs:

Perception

Interpretation

Perspective

Then we will glimpse into what we don't give thought to as that equally determines the quality of our lives.

Happiness is easy to measure. You feel great or you don't. What is on your mind either energizes or depletes you. You could be lying on the couch talking to your friend about how bored and tired you are. You are sure of it because that is how you "feel." A minute later your partner comes in with keys to a new Porsche and says, "Let's take a spin in your new car." Tired no more as you leap across the room.

On occasion, life may appear to be on a steady course, but you can count on the status quo being disrupted and changing at any moment - with a phone call, a pair of keys dangling in front of you, or a newly discovered mindset.

Perception

A personal reality

There is no one diet, religion, sexual preference, political position that is held universally. We all act out our beliefs on the world stage. Each of us is a playwright scripting, casting, directing, and starring in our own production – The World According to Me.

Unbeknownst to us, behind the scenes, our minds run a covert operation. The framework is the same for everyone although the conditions differ. What operates in the back of our minds is a conviction that "Things *should* be a certain way." When things and people don't meet our contrived criteria, we rebel in some fashion.

I cannot overstate how important the conviction that "things are supposed to be like this" is. It is running the show. It chooses the clothes we wear, if we choose to be married or not, if we join a gang, our level of education. Everything. It is at the basis of every argument with yourself and others. We measure everyone in our life against the myth that we've got it right. It's a false structure in which we hold people in contempt when they don't live up to our standards and ideology. I call that a big "mythstake."

The word "should" is a rogue player in the think tank. It informs us how good or bad we or other people are. Growing up, my mother taught me that you "should" never put a bottle of ketchup on the table. It "should" be poured into the glass container with the itty-bitty spoon. This is probably how I got into the luxury hotel game.

Perception is a personal bias, in no way universal, and is formed through our nature, what we were taught, and how we construed life's experiences so far. I promise you not everyone's story of what high school was like is similar although the experience was shared.

Perception carves out our personal and individual reality. How we experience life depends upon how we acquired our world view. Some experience life as suffering. Others have pain but choose not to suffer. For others it is about self-expression, devotion, or joy. From our personal frame of reference our life plays out. It is essential to grasp that perception is a learned view, not actual in any way.

It is invaluable to explore how we acquired our individual mindset. It follows that if we constructed our viewpoints brick by brick, we can deconstruct them the same way if the current blueprint no longer suits us. We will discover that reality is more like clay we get to mold than hard cast concrete.

DISTINCTION:

Bodies tense up when sensing opposition. Understanding this is essential when it comes to relaxing our rigid structures. It is our individual perceptions of reality that are responsible for our point of view on everything. To think differently and reclaim control of our mind are at the helm of raising our happiness quotient.

Blind Spots: The Hidden Bias

What we don't know

Barry Pogorel is a mentor, friend, and world class leadership consultant. I assisted him in seminars on three continents. I will never forget the first time I heard Barry ask a group of leaders, "How would the world occur to you if you were born with blue sunglasses on?" Most answered, "Duh, Barry. Blue."

Barry chuckled without judgement as only he can and said. "Incorrect. The answer is normal." Blue would look normal to you because that's how you perceived the world from the beginning. This is important. Our initial imprint keeps us from recognizing our singular viewpoint contains blind spots.

Initially, as we awaken, it is difficult to look at another point of view because we want to be correct so badly. To perceive our beliefs may be slanted is terrifying to the ego and our sense of right and wrong, but by holding tight to unchallenged points of view, we trade a world of possibility for a teaspoon of certainty.

DISTINCTION:

We all have a bias on how we interpret the world around us – what we refer to as reality. We construct our viewpoint with partial information. The beginning of enlightenment is in realizing the variable nature of things.

Crossing the Great Divide

What is required to grow and expand

We learn something new every day. Timing matters. The student is not always ready for something new. Maybe we grow from a new experience or maybe we discard it. Once in a while we hear or read something new and its profundity literally rocks us and we will never be the same. That was my reaction the first time I read the following quote by William Blake.

"If the doors of perception were cleansed then everything would appear to man as it is, Infinite. For man has closed himself up, till he sees all things through narrow chinks of his cavern."

Blake is saying that our view of the world is a partial one – one slice out of the whole pie. A person growing up in a loving home cannot understand what a homeless person or an orphan goes through. We can't experience every degree of humanity. The best we can do is bring compassion to situations people find themselves in including ourselves.

If we think our current conditions and circumstances are something we are stuck with, that too is a limited view. How we think about things is not random. They are patterns. Once we become aware that automatic patterns are at play, we can take control of where we place our attention. In doing so, we can expect new and exciting options to reveal themselves. Our beliefs are like mud in our eye. We lose sight of infinite expansion and the privileges that personal growth affords us.

In The Republic, one of the more famous works in western philosophy, Plato demonstrates that however the world is presented to us initially is what we conform to despite contrary evidence. In the book there are prisoners that are handcuffed inside a cave. Because they are also unable to turn their heads they can't see there are actual people dancing behind them illuminated by a light source – sun in the day and fire at night. They can only perceive shadows dancing on the wall. The prisoners think the shadows on the wall are absolute reality because that is all they have ever known.

Had one person escaped and seen the sun and dancers for the first time, they would be confused and want to run back to the darkness where they believe the truth lies. The sun pierces his eyes. If he remains outside long enough, his eyes become accustomed to the light. Chances are, however, that he returns to his false world. If not allowed to go back, he will remain reluctant while he progresses to a different understanding.

Plato points out that to progress from believing the cave scene is reality to perceiving something else entirely is difficult and requires education, assistance, and sometimes force. This is us when faced with a new point of view. Before enlightenment comes struggle –

a willingness to see something different. Contradictory input asks us to become a critical thinker. To leave the cave is to question all the cave dweller has ever known. It is easier to remain ignorant than accept a new possibility. Unwilling to step into the light, the prisoners remain passive observers embracing ignorance and loss of freedom over bliss.

DISTINCTION:

Any strongly held belief about the way things are is a version of being born with blue glasses on. Even though we may complain, we are comfortable with the familiarity of our problems and attitudes. We defend them at all costs because to challenge them may imply we have to give a belief structure on which we have built our life and premises on.

Life demands we grow. When we become set in our ways, we contract a sort of rigor mortis of the brain. One day we may wake up to find we were running defense, but we were the only person on the court! Score: 0. No Overtime. To believe that happiness eludes us and favors others based on certain conditions and circumstances is a "chink in the cavern."

On Being Right

Its effect on relationships

People like to be part of a majority because it makes them more certain that they are on the "right" side of things. Needing to be right is a desire to show superiority. Of course, the Catholic Church jailed Galileo in 1633 because he said the earth revolved around the sun which the church did not take kindly to. It took 400 years for the church to reverse their position. Most every great discovery or movement do not have a majority backing them up. A majority doesn't make us right. Just righteous.

In the physical universe and in the animal kingdom there is no right or wrong. Things just are. Three legged dogs aren't judged by other canines. Rain isn't wrong if it soaks your beach wedding. That's nature. When we bring people and egos into the mix let alone a plot of land, right and wrong reign supreme.

In wartime, all sides claim that God is on their side. Methinks that is a made-up rationale to inflict great harm and bend the rules of civility.

You may have had a friend in college who was an environmental advocate. Upon graduation they landed a juicy job with an oil company. You ask her "Are you really going to throw fish and birds under the bus for that bonus check?"

She responds, "I have to make a living." Again, no right or wrong, just rationale.

My friend Holly says I should put on my resume: "Ability to work well with a*holes." The hotel business has its share. I worked for most of them. One of them in particular needed to be right at everyone else's expense.

The company had just taken over a high-end luxury hotel and hired me to be the general manager. My boss came into town and called a meeting. The executive team didn't understand why he didn't approve renewal of a hard to come by and well-earned organic garden certification by the state. Renewal was around $225.00 – a pittance against the cash flow of the hotel that charged over $1,000.00 per night. When Boss poo-pooed the renewal, the whole table got emotional and argued for the importance of the garden to the overall success of the hotel. Boss then called them liars to their faces. It was shocking. Someone mentioned how much the guests loved watching the chef pick ingredients for the evening's repast. As Boss saw it, since chef used ingredients other than those in the garden, our website was based on lies. It was then that the assistant manager looked up from his computer and said, "Boss, you are right. On the website, it does sound like all our food comes from there, but we can make that correction."

Boss responded loudly. "Of course, I'm right. Do you think I don't know that? And yet you challenge me? Get over your silly 'little garden.'"

What was left in the wake of this confrontation was fear, loss of respect both ways and mourning for what could have been. Apparently, that wasn't enough. An hour later, another dark cloud was forming.

It was two days before Christmas. Boss announced there was a problem with the payroll system and, while not their fault, the employees who were overpaid two months ago had to pay down the debt. This was the first we heard of it. He wanted us to announce this before Christmas. It affected the employees making minimum wage who did not realize they were overpaid. I was sure they had spent their paychecks on gifts for their children already and made this known to Boss. The hotel could have underwritten this easily and it would have gone unnoticed. There was no room for negotiation, just a mixed message from him that I should handle the communication appropriately and not make the company look bad. Scrooged. Later, we entertained our corporate colleagues with rounds of tequila at $350 per shot.

Needing to be right all the time is an ego screaming, "Feed me, feed me." It sucks creativity and partnership out of any organization, including romance. How many of us know people that must be right? The boss? The sister who tells her sibling how to live her life? I am sure we all know people who must be the smartest guy in the room. If you need to be right all the time, you may want to consider living alone. Whether you do the dishes or not, you'll always be right. We hurt people and kill off potential when we suppress self-expression.

DISTINCTION:

Being right is the booby prize. Do you really want to not have sex tonight because earlier in the day you argued over GPS directions with your spouse?

There is something to gain and something to be lost when needing to be right all the time. The ego may be tamed for a moment, but future communication suffers a setback. People who feel attacked tend to shut down and go inward.

Husband Dan has a chip on his shoulder about Apple. I am sure the tech world is divided on whether Steve Jobs was a genius or a tyrant. Who is right? Moreover, who cares? I could state how many Apple users there are and make him wrong. Instead, I move gently into the next moment and don't challenge his rant. To dispute him would be my needing to be right and making him wrong. It's his opinion. If I am up for a tug of war, there is a beach I can go to and play. Relationships collapse after so many years of ego tennis. Eventually, someone will serve someone with divorce papers. It just gets tiring.

Often, people give good advice when they suggest we "just let it go." Letting go of something that is bothering you is at odds with needing to be right. Imagine "Letting Go" vs "Being Right" in a boxing match. There are no winners unless beleaguered "Being Right" throws in the towel to "Letting Go" so "Letting Go" can take its much-deserved title.

"I ain't often right
But I've never been wrong
It seldom turns out the way
it does in the song
Once in a while
You get shown the light
In the strangest of places
If you look at it right."

— Scarlet Begonias,
Words by Robert Hunter,
Music by Jerry Garcia,
The Grateful Dead

Carrots and Karats

Am I selling out?

When it comes to work, I recommend working with companies whose values are aligned with yours. I sold my soul a bit to take the hotel job I mentioned earlier because on the outside it was so appealing. But on my inside, it was really appalling.

Before joining that company, almost everyone in the industry I spoke to told me what a difficult company this was to work for, but I count on myself to fit in just about anywhere. Apparently, that is not a safe bet.

During the interview process, I asked the "Chief Culture Officer" about their culture. He responded it was all in the numbers. I politely rephrased, "Yes of course, I can bring that home, but how would you describe your culture?" "The numbers!" he confirmed.

Warning signs continued to pop up. While onboarding, I sent a two-sentence email to Boss and the president of the company thanking them for the opportunity and committed to making them very proud. I received a call from Boss the next day saying: "Why do you write to the president? Just concentrate on your training," and a disconnect tone followed. When I would recount my first five months at the hotel with my closest friend she told me from the time I accepted the position that they treated me terribly. It turns out she was correct, but I continued to make excuses for them. The next eighteen months were a struggle. Not so different entering into a marriage where you have early warning signs.

It was a culture clash, for sure. I tried to go along but I felt as if I couldn't keep the Kool Aid down. I realized that in fact they did have a culture. The culture was "Corporate knows best and we know not to trust any of you." The carrot on the stick was a sizeable paycheck and industry status but that carrot wouldn't have flourished in "little garden."

DISTINCTION:

Years ago, Mama Charlotte shared an anecdote with me. She said, "With the Krupp diamond, you get Mr. Krupp." She was referring to marrying a rich guy you really did not want to be married to, but you fall for the shiny object. It's an old saying but so true. Whether you sell out for carrots or karats, know what you are getting into. Eventually, it will be your nemesis.

As they say, the writing is on the wall. Are we willing to look at it or ignore our gut feeling and predetermine to look away? When we sell out for anything inauthentic, happiness exits… stage left.

Perspective

More than one reality

After several months on planet earth, your mind will encounter a tour guide named Perspective. Like all good guides, Perspective will point out areas of interest and where to place your attention. As you grow, you will adopt Perspective's point of view. Thereafter, whatever you focus on you will get more of. It doesn't matter whether you focus on what is wanted or unwanted.

If you continually perceive something as "the way things are," you will have more experience of it. We attract what we think about. It is that simple.

Happiness is an inside job. It is just under the surface of our everyday preoccupations ready to emerge glorious if we let it. It depends entirely on your perspective on the future, regardless of how you got yourself to where you stand today. If you think you need to have that certain something to be happy, expect to receive fool's gold. If you wish for more money you may find a penny in the taxi. Again, your perspective determines what you pay attention to.

If time is spent focusing on a dwindling bank balance, less will arise as the dominant perspective, and make it difficult for us to pay attention to what else pleases us. If the size of your bank account looks small, so will the rest of the world. Wishing for more money is the same vibration as I don't have enough. Lack begets lack. Sensing the bounty around you in nature, the arts, in kindness, sets you up to receive more. Everything is just for now. Your bank account will appreciate when you become appreciative.

Words don't matter. Your energy about things is what makes the difference – your vibe. That's why specific affirmations don't work when your bank balance makes you anxious. You straight up don't believe it. When you cultivate desire for a new future, whether it's a trip to Fiji or money to move out of a current situation, create non-specific statements you can align with such as.

I observe abundance everywhere and can see it for me too. I am grateful for what I have today, and all that I desire that is on its way. Thank you. I am open to receive this or better.

Then start living as if. You can go to a diner and see a fried egg on a plate or you can look at the same egg and see a sun emerging from the clouds. Perspective is not only your tour guide, but bus driver as well. It will take you to see the places you have already seen, unless you direct it elsewhere.

Become rigorous and strategic about what you think. By that I mean, focus on the solution, not the problem or story. I heard a woman on a talk show say, "I just seem to attract the bad boys."

Note the belief system is "attract bad boys" as if it's carved in stone and not in thought.

Neuroscientists agree there are about eleven million bits of information we could tune into each second, but we only perceive about sixteen of them. For instance, without my bringing your attention to it, are you aware of how your thigh feels upon the chair or couch you are resting on? The indent the watch made on your wrist? The sound of the air conditioning vent? These elements are acting upon us, but our limited awareness is focused elsewhere. Thank goodness for our autonomic nervous system. Otherwise we would eat a cookie and have to remember to supply the saliva, the swallow response, the trip down the throat, the acid in the stomach.... you get the picture. There is a lot going on we don't pay attention to.

When I drive by a boutique, I am drawn to the window display. My husband, in the same car at the same time doesn't even see the boutique, would think it a waste of time and money to walk through the door, and doesn't think I "need" anything else. This from a man who owns three pairs of shoes including sneakers. What does "need" have to do with anything? Perspective!

Witness how diverse personal interpretation is as it affects something as simple and "realistic" as defining a tree. We can all agree the tree we are observing may be so many feet tall, primarily brown, roots in earth, deciduous, etcetera. That is a visual field (and how do I know what I call brown appears the same to you?)

Adding our personal perspective is much more nuanced than we think. This is how a tree appears in different perspectives. A tree is:

Logger: Lumber and money to put food on the table

Painter: Beauty, strength, a source of splintered sunlight

Bird: Home and a place to raise babies

Squirrel: A place to hide and stash dinner

Child: Something to climb and boast about

Scientist: An ecosystem for birds and animals

Firefighter: Dangerous tinder

Environmentalist: Sacred and ancient soul of the earth – to be protected at all costs

DISTINCTION:

What we believe is nothing more than a product of thinking the same thoughts over and over. Those thoughts solidify into beliefs and become the foundation and structure on which we build our lives.

Conscious awakening begins when we can appreciate another perspective to be valid even if it is inconsistent with our own. This is a wake-up call not to be missed. Judgement of ourselves or others causes stress and anxiety – the opposite of happiness. To consider other points of view as legitimate relaxes our uptight structures and makes us more easygoing. Perspective alters the notion of one absolute reality. Wobbly, isn't it?

Because we are the ones that adopt and create our beliefs we can change them. Beliefs are not a thing. They are a *think*. We are what we think. We live the lives we believe we deserve. If we are not living a life we love, it's time to consult our bus driver to visit someplace new.

"Good morning. This is your wake-up call. The sun will be shining all day and so will you. Don't pass on it. Pass it on."

Imagine yourself with no beliefs. What would you choose to believe in?

"While we have the gift of life, it seems to me the only tragedy is to allow part of us to die – whether it is our spirit, our creativity or our glorious uniqueness. There is no real security except for whatever you build inside yourself."

— Gilda Radner

Interpretation

The architect of your life

Thank you, Perception and Perspective. Now along comes Interpretation.

Once we perceive anything via our thoughts and five senses, we automatically interpret those sensations. We determine our personal universe through interpretation. It is the master informer and designer of our individual perspective. There is not a thought, argument, war, or piece of art that isn't the product of interpretation. Even judges with the same law books arrive at different interpretations affecting someone's entire future.

Without exception, everything that occurs to us is based upon what we tell ourselves is happening, facts be damned. A woman called up a talk show saying her boyfriend broke up with her. Her question for the host was, "Should I leave him?" She did not interpret that this was a moot question. In needing to be in control, she ignored the fact he already moved on.

I recommended Dan see the movie Three Billboards Outside Ebbing, Missouri. I told him the film was hysterical. His response to me after seeing the movie was "How could you say that was funny? That was tragic." Interpretation is our personal umpire.

We make everything up. We make up state lines, voting districts, how to dress for each occasion. We follow religious rules or bend them to our discretion, or someone comes along to create a version of that religion with dumbed down requirements. Do you interpret having a celebration as a crime against nature? Some religions do.

Interpretation even triumphs over scientific facts on climate change when the facts are economically inconvenient. Make no mistake. How you interpret things affects everything in your life, including the ability to be happy.

I was running a resort in Tucson that at the time was the number one destination resort in North America. I was brought in to drive business results and lower costs while maintaining the integrity of the experience. I had thirteen employees in the yoga department. I brought them together to discuss how we could keep everyone working but not all in yoga. Their interpretation was that I was here to destroy the resort. I interpreted that the yoga team was "not flexible!" The important thing to note here is if you are leading a team or attempting to get a point across, everyone will interpret it differently. It is advantageous to ask people how they interpreted what you said so you may clear up misunderstandings early.

It doesn't pay to get angry at someone who misunderstands what you say. It's just interpretation at play. I once complained to my dad that I was the lowest paid general manager at Hilton. I was looking for sympathy and justification when he answered, "Nanci, somebody has to be." That man could always make me laugh.

The reason communication is so difficult in all aspects of our lives is because of how we interpret everything.

A couple of hotels back, we held an Employee Opinion Survey. As usual, no matter what hotel we were at, my colleagues and I always received a very poor rating on communication. I was determined to change this metric, especially since I went out of my way to attend daily pre-shift meetings, set up weekly and monthly meetings with teams, create open forums, newsletters, open door, etc. After receiving the poor rating, I began every meeting and conversation by saying, "Good morning, team. This is communication." I would close the meetings with "Thank you for the robust conversations. That was communication." It helped. A lot. Some associates interpreted a lack of communication in the entire hotel just because they didn't get a day off they requested. It seems to me we are all very self-involved galaxies, spinning around and bumping into each other now and again.

Communication is tricky, but less so when you are aware of the implications of interpretation and get in front of them.

DISTINCTION:

Interpretation is the architect of our lives. We translate our interpretations into our feelings and behaviors. The way we feel is *always* self-generated. Feelings don't exist outside of us. I was at a Tony Award winning show and the woman next to me took out her tissues and told me she expected to cry a lot. On several occasions, people were silently sobbing around me. I could see the protagonist's dilemma but I wasn't near a tear. We are the interpreter, umpire and generator of all things we call "me."

Perhaps one night, you will sit with a glass of wine and wonder, "What did I interpret today?" The answer is "Everything." Then ask, "If I looked at things differently, how might I turn the situations that bother me to my advancement?"

Happiness Assassins

Be on the lookout

Worry

Many of us have a tough time mentally "being present"- experiencing the current moment free from thought. Once we attempt to capture that moment in speaking or thinking about it, that moment has already vanished. We then find our minds either wandering off into the future or rolling back to the past.

I know one thing for sure. If I am worried, I am not in present awareness. Worry is a future based version of interpretation. It is hope turned inside out - a projection of what you don't want to have happen. Worry sticks its neck out into the future. Happiness can only be enjoyed in the present moment.

When you are happy, you experience peace. The Buddhists say that "pain is inevitable, but suffering is a choice." We do more damage in our minds than the actual events call for. You don't need a therapist to let go of limiting beliefs or suffering. Every moment is an opportunity to let go of a thought and come back to peace.

I was on a road trip with my girlfriends. One of them started talking about a past love that haunted her thoughts. She laid it out like this: "One part of me understands it is over, another part of me wants to try again, and yet another part of me…." I suggested what she calls parts is merely indecision. I asked her to consider there are no parts, just thoughts. This one, then this one, then this one. You can't send a part of you into a relationship – not a happy one, anyway.

Doubt

Doubt is a killer of dreams coming true. If you want to attract anything into your life, doubt is a dragon that must and can be slayed. It is yet another interpretation you can control. If you can talk yourself into doubting something, you can just as easily talk yourself into believing it can happen. Life is nothing but uncertain and that's the good news. Maybe not as expedient as advice from a fortune cookie, but with practice, it is as easy to take a leap of faith as it is a leap of doubt. Doubt means you are focused on the problem, not the solution.

Doubt is the opposite of conviction. I know of a young girl who, despite a lot of competition, was determined to get into a certain college. She told her family she sent applications to several colleges, but actually only applied to her one target.

She was accepted.

She came from a family that taught her conviction brought about desired results. For her, having Plan B was out of the question. To have a Plan B was a fallback and defied conviction. (Disclaimer: Not recommended for diversifying your financial portfolio!)

Jumping to Conclusions

Imagine you are at a restaurant looking forward to a quiet dinner. Children at the next table are making all sorts of noise and jumping around. Their mother appears distracted and isn't doing a thing to quiet them down. Before you call for the manager, you clear your throat and say, "Ma'am, isn't there anything you can do to keep your children (thinking "brats") a bit quieter?" The woman looks at you and apologizes. "Oh! I am so sorry. We just came from the hospital. Their grandfather died today. We were all very close. I didn't realize. I am so sorry."

You may still change tables, but your viewpoint has most likely turned from anger to compassion. (Better for digestion).

Information reframes how we interpret situations. How often do we interpret people and situations to be wrong when we know so little about them?

"All things are subject to interpretation. Whichever interpretation prevails at a given time is a function of power and not truth."

— Fredrich Nietzsche

Oh, the Memories

A complicated and mercurial processor

At one time or another we have all sworn that we heard or saw something one way but someone else is telling us it didn't happen like that. Occasionally, I will ask my husband a question. Dan will tell me he told me that already. I figure he thinks he told me, but I don't recall it. Maybe he thought about telling me. Who knows? Maybe Alexa.

Neurologists who study memory say we fill in gaps unconsciously. Eyewitness testimony is hugely influential in criminal cases, yet brain research has proven again and again that human memory is unreliable. Likewise, most times we retell stories the details are subject to embellishment and change. (How large was that fish?)

Memory is a complicated system which I will leave to the scientists. It's the stories we tell each other that fascinate me. Illusion and reality are closely bound up in our personal world.

The other day, I was going through pictures with a girlfriend. She remarked, "That's when we were in New Orleans." I said, "You were never in New Orleans with me or anyone else. This photo was taken of us in Atlanta."

Recently, I was streaming a live concert held in upstate New York in the late 1970's. I was feeling very nostalgic for that time in my life and all the fun I had. I called two friends who I recalled going to the concert with and asked, "I know how we got there but how did we got home?"

They both replied, "We never went to Watkins Glen so getting home was never a problem."

In fact, we did see the same bands two months earlier in Washington DC, but the illusion we saw them again in New York occurred to me like a real memory just the same.

Another time a friend and I drove from Boulder, Colorado to Aspen overnight for a day of whitewater rafting. We quietly opened the front door of his friend's home at three in the morning and snuck into the guest room. We were awakened several hours later by a cheery man who opened the door and asked, "Do you want pancakes? And by the way, *who are you*?" We were in the wrong house. What is even funnier is I had a girlfriend tell the story years later as if it happened to her.

Let's not even get into the faulty memory at trials where people's lives are at stake.

DISTINCTION:

Best not to argue with someone about what was said or what happened because unless it is on tape, in complete context, all our memories are fallible at best. Allow misunderstandings to be just that and start anew.

Soak up pleasure from the memories you love. If you dredge up a memory that feels like a black cloud hanging over you, it is. Release it before it drains your life force in the now.

Whatever we think about becomes our present point of attraction regardless if it occurred thirty years ago. If it feels good, take a "Blissbath" in it. If not, get out of the water. It is shark infested.

In the Beginning

Earliest imprints

As newborns, we come into the world very needy. We miss "womb service" which was all the rage during gestation. Stunned by unfamiliar light and sounds, we can't express to you what is happening to us, so we hope you read a few books before this event.

Newborns cry because they don't have language to express themselves. Without a brain developed enough for language, personal identity cannot exist. There is just sensory exchange in the oneness of all things. There is no separation of self until we learn the meaning of "you" and "me." Once a child understands that their road to becoming a separate self begins. They learn to assert themselves to get their needs met. "Love me. Feed me. Stay with me. I'm cold." Language begins as a survival mechanism. As we develop, we can use language as a precursor to great joy or remain in survival mode, attempting to manipulate the world to conform to our base needs.

Without language, there can be no paradox.

We are exposed to an education process that teaches us everything except what is necessary to become an evolved and fulfilled human being. One must travel off the beaten path to acquire those skills. Without critical observation, most of us react to stimuli and continue to apply the same skill set to tackle today's issues that we developed as children. That is why, regardless of the situation, we go through life complaining about the same things, ad nauseum. "Nobody loves me. No one understands me. Show me you care." Consistent complaining is our psyche's way of telling us our modus operandi is due for a tune-up.

DISTINCTION:

The enlightenment process begins when we become the observer of our habitual thought patterns. Once we begin to witness how our thoughts originate and why we think what we think, we can become objective about them and then modify and control them.

"It seems to me that before we set out on a journey to find reality, to find God, before we can act, before we can have any relationship with another . . . it is essential that we begin to understand ourselves first."

— Krishnamurti

Meet the Enneagram
(Pronounced Any-a-gram)

Who are we really?

Do you ever get restless? Have thoughts that something is missing? Maybe it feels like general dissatisfaction or a sense that there is more. A typical antidote is to fill that hole with stuff, search for the perfect relationship, work your ass off, buy the motorcycle. However, after we put yet another notch on our achievement belt, we fail to rid ourselves of a sense of lack, incompleteness. That is the time to take the journey inward.

One of the more provocative courses of study I have ever pursued is The Enneagram. It is an ancient teaching system that sought to uncover the question, "Who am I, really?"

I offer you a taste of it here as it is life changing and it doesn't hurt or cost money to learn about it. The enneagram offers a method of discovery that provides in depth insight into nine personality types (also referred to as self or ego). It outlines what each type is preoccupied with and how we interact with personalities that see the world different than we do.

The study of the enneagram reveals certain patterns of thinking and behaving we assumed as children to make our survival certain. Unconsciously, thoughts of the nine different types might take the form of, "If I get good grades and am perfect, Mommy will love me; If I am quiet, Daddy won't leave; If I take care grandpa, I will be needed; If I am different, I will be noticed." Adopting an instinctual motivation at a young age becomes the framework for how we make our choices as adults. Emotionally, each type shows variations of anger, fear, or shame to defend and protect ourselves.

Unlike other personality profiles that put you in a box and leave you there, by understanding the limitations of the type we identify with, we can grow into higher levels of consciousness and turn neuroses into awareness. Living without discovery and insight to our very nature, people experience blocks to their full potential and freedom. There is nothing more difficult to overcome than an antagonist that remains obscured.

The Nine Personality Types

Where do I fit in?

I encourage everyone to pick up a book on the enneagram or take a gander online. It is mind blowing in its depth and implications for living a life you love. What I have outlined below is a tip of the iceberg take on the nine archetypes. The Enneagram is used widely in business, spiritual traditions, and psychology. When I worked for the groundbreaking company Kimpton Hotels and Restaurants, it was the basis of our culture. Everyone in a leadership position had to understand the frame of reference for each type. As such, Kimpton launched the lifestyle and boutique hotel craze blazing a path in the industry no one had gone down before.

The Enneagram Institute (one of many schools of the enneagram) lays out the most notable characteristics of the types below. I included the unconscious childhood messages that have a profound effect on our growing identity. (Wisdom of the Enneagram – Don Richard Russo and Ross Hudson).

For fun, I have added famous people and dog breeds that appear to fit the profiles.

Type One: The Performer:

The Rational, Idealistic Type: Principled, Purposeful, Self-Controlled, and Perfectionistic.

Unconscious Childhood Message:
"It's not okay to make mistakes." vs. "You are good."

Famous: Joan of Arc, Pope John Paul II, Margaret Thatcher, "Mr. Spock."

Dog: Poodle

Type Two: The Helper

The Caring, Interpersonal Type: Demonstrative, Generous, People-Pleasing, and Possessive.

Unconscious Childhood Message:
"It's not okay to have your own needs." vs. "You are wanted."

Famous: Mother Teresa, Archbishop Desmond Tutu, Tin Woodsman in The Wizard of Oz.

Dog: Labrador

Type Three: The Achiever

The Success-Oriented, Pragmatic Type: Adaptive, Excelling, Driven, and Image conscious.

Unconscious Childhood Message:
"It's not okay to have your own feelings
and identity." vs. "You are loved for yourself.

Famous: Bill Clinton, Tom Cruise, Tony Robbins

Dog: Jack Russell

Type Four: The Individualist

The Sensitive, Withdrawn Type: Expressive, Dramatic, Self-Absorbed, and Temperamental.

Unconscious Childhood Message:
"It's not okay to be too functional
or too happy." vs. "You are seen for who you are."

Famous: Michael Jackson, Rudolf Nureyev, Bob Dylan

Dog: Chihuahua

Type Five: The Investigator

The Intense, Cerebral Type: Perceptive, Innovative, Secretive, and Isolated.

Unconscious Childhood Message:
"It's not okay to be comfortable in the world." vs. "Your needs are not a problem."

Famous: Bill Gates, Albert Einstein, Stephen Hawking

Dog: Border Collie

Type Six: The Loyalist

The Committed, Security-Oriented Type: Engaging, Responsible, Anxious, and Suspicious.

Unconscious Childhood Message:
"It's not okay to trust yourself." vs. "You are safe."

Famous: Tom Hanks, Bruce Springsteen, Princess Diana, Woody Allen

Dog: Bullmastiff

Type Seven: The Enthusiast

The Busy, Fun-Loving Type: Spontaneous, Versatile, Distractible, and Scattered.

Unconscious Childhood Message:
"It's not okay to depend on anyone
for anything." vs. "You will be taken care of."

Famous: John F. Kennedy, Robin Williams, Jim Carrey, Steven Spielberg

Dog: Golden Retriever

Type Eight: The Challenger

The Powerful, Dominating Type: Self-Confident, Decisive, Willful, and Confrontational.

Unconscious Childhood Message:
"It's not okay to be vulnerable or to
trust anyone." vs. "You will not be betrayed."

Famous: Martin Luther King, Jr., Franklin Delano Roosevelt, Pablo Picasso, Marlon Brando

Dog: Rottweiler

Type Nine: The Peacemaker

The Easygoing, Self-Effacing Type: Receptive, Reassuring, Agreeable, and Complacent.

Unconscious Childhood Message:
"It's not okay to assert yourself." vs. "Your presence matters.

Famous: Abraham Lincoln, Joseph Campbell, Whoopi Goldberg, Walt Disney

Dog: Bernese Mountain Dog

Everyone is looking for a way to be more fulfilled and how to best navigate their journey. The wisdom the enneagram affords us has everything to do with cultivating peace, a life you love, and exponentially expanding your potential.

When I first discovered I was clearly a Type Seven, I couldn't believe how identical the description of me was. I always figured my thoughts and proclivities were mine and mine alone. Never did I have any idea that an archetype of me existed and billions shared my overall perspective on things. Carl Jung was a student of the enneagram and spoke extensively on the collective unconscious not just for the human species but the individual types.

DISTINCTION:

Understanding your enneagram type is a first step to real freedom. If your mind is the lockbox, this is the key. It is a stepping stone to leading to greater levels of peace, happiness, and consciousness.

To approach the enneagram is to travel a road inward. Understanding what motivates us and others offers us insight into to how people think and what is behind their behavior. That awareness vastly improves communication, solidifies teams and families, and calls forth much needed compassion toward others.

To recognize the value of the enneagram cannot be overstated.

Examples of The Enneagram at Work in my Life

Why most self-help books don't self help

BUSINESS

At a typical staff meeting, I would suggest something new for us to accomplish, only to bump into eight other points of view on why it would or wouldn't work. Most staff meetings have people wondering what the other people in the room are smoking. Understanding the enneagram has allowed my teams and me to produce results quickly and in alignment.

MARRIAGE

I don't think I would ever have married my husband without knowledge of what drives him to be the way he is. Dan is Type Eight. Also known as The Challenger, The Protector, The Boss. Eights are powerful and dominating. Control is important to them. The world occurs as things being fair or unfair. They are decisive, black and white thinkers. They are given to anger very easily and don't recognize how their anger affects others. I am completely opposite. Not better. Opposite. Once I understood how Type

Eights think and operate, I could accept him and the amazing traits that Eights possess (though unavailable at first glance).

I'd still be in the bar or Match.com if it weren't for the enneagram.

STRANGERS

I recall a seminar in Berkeley with Helen Palmer, one of the eminent thought leaders on the subject today. Helen had a representative of each type onstage and interviewed us to see how different types respond to the same situation. I will never forget when Type Four (The Romantic, The Individualist) spoke. I thought, "Oh my God, she is *sooooo* dramatic and sorrowful." Type Four turned to me after I spoke and said, "How can you be so shallow? Life is difficult." We clearly had a different bias on things, but we build our lives based upon that point of view. Figuratively, did you ever want to bonk someone on the side of the head when they couldn't see your point of view? The enneagram will relieve that frustration.

Dan and I were dining with my boss and his wife one evening. Somehow, the conversation drifted to whether we weigh ourselves or not. I bring this up to demonstrate how much influence our type has on our most simple behaviors.

Nanci. (The Enthusiast, Type Seven) "I never get on a scale unless I think that I am going to like the results. I don't want to receive 'bad' news." (Sevens run their lives avoiding pain and limitation).

Boss' Wife: (The Perfectionist, Type One) "I weigh myself every day. If I am not at my perfect weight, I beat myself up and become very critical, but I need to know where I stand." (Ones have a very critical and judgmental nature of themselves and others).

Boss: (The Loyalist, Type Six) "I get on the scale to check out if I need to see a doctor to watch my weight. I don't always trust the scale. Maybe I should get a second opinion. (Type Six suffers from a lack of confidence and trust).

Dan: (The Boss, Type Eight) "Who cares if my weight is up or down. Doesn't matter to me." (Type Eight are decisive and direct and speak from their gut).

You could say that without awareness of your type's bias, you can never get enough of what you don't really want. For example, if I am driven to be successful in business in order to feel self-worth, I will always push to succeed regardless of consequences to health, family and lifestyle. The enneagram invites us to observe hidden and outdated motivations, so we may let go of troublesome and unwanted behavior and habits. In a word, it is freedom!

DISTINCTION:

I am going to let a secret out of the bag. There is a reason self-help books rarely work. Affirmations, how to books, have no ability to change imprinted patterns we are unaware of. We act out of our paradigm as if in a trance. We will continue to have the same arguments with our loved ones when we don't understand them or ourselves. That is why there are thousands of self-help books out there and few make a difference. We can't heal a wound we don't see. It is only when we can acknowledge what hinders us that we can move toward a more fulfilling future. The enneagram offers us greater clarity on all interpersonal dynamics.

"Look to the future,
because that is where
you'll spend the
rest of your life."

— George Burns

Your Brain on "Croc"

Do we really have free will?

Deep inside our skulls dwell the same type of reptile complex found in a crocodile. Even after tens of millions of years of evolution our reptilian brain is still the source of our "fight or flight" response. What Daniel Goleman refers to in his book Emotional Intelligence as an "amygdala hijack," it is an intense emotional response to stimuli out of proportion to the threat. Fear and anger come to the rescue when we feel threatened. However, these days our lizard brain is more concerned with imagined threats to our ego. Someone disagreeing with us should not have the same effect as a brontosaurus showing up at our cave door, but you wouldn't know it given how quickly tempers and emotions flair when our ego cries, "Foul!"

Inside our "croc" brain, we process unconsciously and instinctively. Years ago, our preoccupations revolved around food, shelter, sex, and safety. These days our brain defaults to black and white thinking, fast formed assumptions, and generalizations just to keep up with the onslaught of data coming at us. It is this unconscious sorting that carves physical ruts in our thinking patterns.

DISTINCTION:

Thinking, like breathing, is automatic but we do have the power to control both. When you find yourself in a situation that makes you uncomfortable, it is good to have priorities. Your happiness is such a priority.

To react is to fall back on predictable patterns. To act with choice in the moment is to be powerfully aware and conscious. When I was young and my mom would instruct me to pull my hair back off my face, I took offense setting up a pattern to avoid criticism at all costs. Now I just embrace having a mom here.

Always keep in mind what you want as an outcome in any given situation. Did you really want to insult the representative at the boarding gate because the flight was delayed three hours. Did it help? Let your desires dictate your future rather than imaginary fear and threats to your ego.

"Ruts up, Doc?"

Reprogramming the brain

There is a myth that the streets of Boston are laid out so chaotically because the original city planners wanting to pave the roads, followed the ruts the cows formed over the past hundreds of years. The term "don't follow the cow path" is still used in technology today denoting there are more effective and efficient ways to think about things other than memorializing makeshift solutions.

The same goes for how our minds form neuron pathways that become habits. Even though alternatives are plentiful, we are habitual creatures that go down the road most traveled.

As with everything, there are positive and negative outcomes. The first time you burn your hand on the stove, you build a pathway to avoid that. Good. If we have a difficult confrontation as a child, we may do everything we can in the future to avoid confrontation. Not as good.

Any time we practice a new thought, we initiate a new route in our brain. We have neural pathways for sweets to reward ourselves, for preferred sexual proclivities, how we behave at work, at home, how disciplined we are. I do not have a pathway for getting on a treadmill, but I do have one for dance classes. I must dance. Developing an ability to sit still for meditation is an acquired pathway. I do it because of the value I receive, not because I particularly like stopping my momentum. Our general program is to always be thinking thoughts we always think. Meditation disrupts that by creating space for new and creative thoughts to swim by.

We already have neural connections that make us serial worriers or ones that bring up past injustices. There is also a neural rut for beating ourselves up. Misery is not on the happiness scale.

If you have a pathway that wants carrot cake (reward) every day after lunch, and your desire is to lose a few pounds, consider you can create a new physical pathway in your brain. This is science. Try half a slice, then two bites, etc... Eventually, you will build a connection from the brain to the body where you are satisfied with less.

Shifts begin with new ways of thinking. For instance, consider a mantra such as, "There are foods for the mouth and foods for the stomach." Then use your imagination. Perhaps begin visualizing which foods belong where. I always thought doughnut sounded too much like "do not" to eat them. As I bring them up to my mouth, all I can think of is, "Do not." Become your own think tank.

DISTINCTION:

There is an upside to complaining. When you recognize complaining for what it is, something you don't want, you could see it as a seed for change. Inside every complaint is a request for a new desire to be fulfilled.

If I decide, "I don't want X anymore," that is a complaint. I could stop there and wallow in the complaint or ask myself, "What do I want?" "Oh, Y would be nice." Good. Now we are getting somewhere. The next question should be, "What is stopping me?" Let's say I come up with several obstacles such as, "I don't have enough money, I need a degree for that, my father will disapprove," consider the following:

For a million dollars, would that obstacle still prevent you from taking action?

What would you tell your best friend to do in the same situation?

Are you blaming anyone for your inability to move forward?

What do you need to have happen to move forward?

What is one baby step you can take?

We are only as limited as our beliefs and lack of imagination.

We need protection as a child. We need expansion as an adult. Life demands we grow and rewards us with a life we love and live out loud.

Happiness: If not now, when?

Undressing the Self - Wrap Up

Setting sail to "free"

I hope you are not chilly now that we have stripped down how we got to be who we are today. Our intention is to lighten the load.

While attending university, I lived in a small mountain town, experiencing the zeitgeist of the late 1970's in every way. The town's motto was "Get Naked and Run Wild." That's what I am asking you to do now. If you love your life, stay the course. If you don't wake up and go to sleep happy and enthusiastic, what follows is an opportunity to strip off what you no longer wish to don.

Recap: Our current imprint is based upon what we were taught as children and then we continued to think and behave based upon that paradigm. It structured how we fit into the world and how we think people, institutions, and the world should conform.

It's not necessarily true. We are influenced by perception, belief (opinion), interpretation, and million years old survival mechanisms. We can see that patterns of thinking, reaction, and behavior surface whether they are called for or not. They become the basis of our decision-making process, and our choices are inextricably connected to our sense of joy and well-being.

Do you know what you want? Can you articulate it? If not specifically, can you identify with the feelings you would love to experience day after day? If the world is not delivering what you ordered and planned for, it is time to examine where the obstacles lie. Have faith. You don't have to see faith to have it.

Freedom, please. Next!

FREEDOM: THE ART OF LETTING GO

Inside the Court of Happiness

Becoming the judge and jury of your life

Imagine you are standing in front of a judge in the Happiness Court of Appeals in The Ninth District. You present your case. All the reasons why life won't let you be happy.

The judge asks you to bring in Life as a witness. No one shows up. There is no one outside of you to blame. You beg the judge for mercy. "Please don't sentence me to a life I don't want."

The judge responds, "We are all born with a death sentence. We know not when it calls. You are the only one in this court that can commute the interim to a life you love. Don't live your life as if you are on probation. The only one you need to report to is yourself. Case dismissed."

DISTINCTION:

We are the defendant, judge and jury in our lives. We could live freely and unencumbered. It is up to us alone.

"Folks are usually about as happy as they make their minds up to be."

— Abraham Lincoln

Bliss or Blisters?

We are living today based on our thoughts of yesterdays

Chances are if life feels more like blisters today, it will feel that way tomorrow as well. Being happy begins with making a commitment that goes something like this:

"My purpose is to be happy. I know I am happy when I feel good. I have control over what I think about. How I feel now will roll over into all my tomorrows bringing more and more satisfaction."

It is said that water seeks its own level. The same is true for us. Once we have realized our happiness potential and that we are the captain of that ship, when we fall short we will be eager to get back to it. We will roll over anything that stands in our way, including our old thought patterns.

How you feel is your compass. Your true north. Applying the tenets I've laid out, you will experience happiness as your new set point.

Bliss begets bliss. Other than the benefit of feeling great right now, if you need a reason to start watching your moods and thoughts, no one says it any better than Abraham-Hicks: "You cannot have a happy ending to an unhappy journey."

If you tell yourself, "I'll be happy when this week is over, after my arm heals, after my divorce," that becomes a life pattern. Obstacles just keep on coming. It is presence of mind in this moment and this day that lead to the events that unfold tomorrow. Everything is a vibration and like attracts like. Misery loves company and joy riders find joy.

DISTINCTION:

We attract to ourselves a tomorrow based on our consciousness today. Period. The future is predicated on the now. There is no pot at the end of the rainbow. The rainbow and the pot are one.

"I, not events, have the power to make me happy or unhappy today. I can choose which it shall be. Yesterday is dead, tomorrow hasn't arrived yet. I have just one day, today, and I'm going to be happy in it."

— Groucho Marx

Because or Be Cause

Being in action or making excuses is a matter of one space

The question "Why?" is usually answered with, "Because." Because is a reason based explanation of why or why not something will happen.

Literally, as I am writing this, my mom called me for a review on a certain movie. I said "Great film. Must be seen."

She responded, "I don't know."

I asked, "Why?"

"Because it is Sunday and it's playing at such a small theatre, we may not get in. Parking is always a problem."

I said "Go early. It's an indie film. I can't imagine the immediate world is standing on line there."

Notice what comes after use of the word "because."

We may use it as a simple matter of fact response: "Because I am exhausted." It also may be a predictor of an outcome based on something that happened long ago: "I couldn't find parking there once."

When I was as kid and we were driving around looking for a parking spot, my mom would inevitably mention how difficult parking was. I recall my dad's response, "Charlotte, we haven't had to take the car in with us yet." Perhaps you have fallen into rut response: "Parking is always a problem." I know of a couple who live in Manhattan sitting on a beach in the Caribbean wondering if they were missing out on a good spot in front of their building BECAUSE they always think about that.

Even one past event can determine our future responses. My girlfriend refuses to shop at the best market in her area. When I asked her why, she said, "Because I don't like the parking there."

I thought, "What? Don't these cars ever go home? Change spaces?"

Eavesdrop on yourself. Make sure your own thought process isn't an obstacle to getting what you really want as in, "Carlos, I love you but I can't marry you because I am commitment phobic." Really? Let's look at that for what it really is. How often do we let pop psychological gobbledygook foil our chances in life? Remember, distinctions matter. Commitment phobic is a cover up phrase. Living a life you love demands clarity so you really know if something is an obstacle or not. Maybe she means, "I've never been married before." So? "I'm vegan and you're paleo." So? Creating distinctions allow us to eliminate obstacles and summon opportunity.

To be cause refers to someone who makes things happen and doesn't wait around for Mercury to get out of retrograde. To be cause is to take charge of your life, your happiness.

DISTINCTION:

The difference between "because" and being cause is use of imagination. When you imagine, you don't have reasons. You are creating out of nothing. Imagination has to do with the future, not the past. Use your imagination daily to consider what you want to have in your life.

Ob"stuck"les

Are they really there?

The misspelling is completely on purpose because obstacles are what keep us stuck. We see them as the reason we can't move the needle. It is our very thoughts or thoughts about our thoughts that become our obstacles.

When is an obstacle not an obstacle? When we acknowledge that something is in the way of having what we want. Usually, reasons just sound "reasonable" to us and we don't question them. They are just there as if they are as real as the chair I am sitting on. Ask any dog facing a bone on the other side of a fence. One way or another, you, like Fido, can get probably get around it.

Whenever I would take over a hotel, I would meet with the executive team. I always ended the discussion with "At the end of our time together, we will have either reasons or results."

We were able to achieve the results we wanted in every single hotel I led. I always thought, "Why didn't the last team accomplish what we did?" There's only one answer. They had "reasons" things couldn't work out, stories why the competition was fierce. It's the same with life. At the end, or in the middle, we will have reasons things aren't working out or results we are proud of and love.

I often check in with myself in all manner of work, family, friends, travel, fun. I am always considering if I am getting what I want out of my life. Everything we have achieved today is based upon previous choices. We may have been stopped by our reasons or may have gone ahead anyway despite them. Either way, here we are.

Before we allow reasons to take our greatest hopes hostage, the question we all need to ask ourselves any time we have to make a choice is "Am I using reasons, excuses, or justification as an obstacle to getting what I really want? If so, what are they and what can I do about them?" We want to be honest so years down the line, we can avoid looking at our life with regret because we didn't learn to leap.

The big five obstacles are usually found around: Family. Health. Work. Finance. Relationships. Consider if the sacrifices they demand of you are necessary or are you living someone else's version of you.

It's important to be truthful. It is possible to create the circumstances you want to have. Oprah Winfrey didn't look around at her life of poverty in Mississippi and see her circumstances as obstacles.

Start with small adjustments. Read the word "nowhere" and now pronounce it "now here." What a difference a space makes!

George Bernard Shaw's quote is spot on: "The reasonable man adapts himself to the world: the unreasonable one persists in trying to adapt the world to himself. Therefore, all progress depends on the unreasonable man."

Shaw isn't referring to an irrational fool. He means a person who doesn't let reasons get in the way of what they want to have happen. JFK had no reason to believe we could send a man to the moon when the technology did not even exist. But we did even though he never lived to see it. He was being "cause."

DISTINCTION:

Make choices from what you really, really want. If there is something you want and don't currently experience, look for the "real" or imagined obstacle. Crack it open like an egg. See what needs unscrambling. If the window won't open, try the door. If opportunity doesn't knock, install a doorbell. If no one answers, walk on.

"Stop waiting until you finish school, until you go back to school, until you lose ten pounds, until you gain ten pounds, until you have kids, until your kids leave the house, until you start work, until you retire, until you get married, until you get divorced, until Friday night, until Sunday morning, until you get a new car or home, until your car or home is paid off, until spring, until summer, until fall, until winter, until you are off welfare, until the first or fifteenth, until your song comes on, until you've had a drink, until you've sobered up, until you die, until you are born again to decide that there is no better time than right now to be happy."

— Anonymous

The Present That Doesn't Belong in a Box

How to generate new ways of thinking

Colloquially, to be "in the box" refers to our inability to think beyond what we already "know."

I cut my teeth at Hilton Hotels as one of the first female general managers in the company. I recall a meeting to instruct all general managers to "Think outside the box." Or, as the president of Hilton once put it: "We need you all to think outside of the box. Except for Sherman." I suppose creativity can be pretty scary for a "box-er." Did they think I might suggest removing the front desk? I did.

Telling people to think out of the box is like saying, "Share something you don't even know you know yet." To think outside the box is to uncover new perspectives. The reason it is difficult for people to get out is we don't realize we *are* the box! Asking most of us to think differently is like asking a fish to comment on the water. They don't even know they are in the water!

Our enneagram type is our box. Recognizing it is freedom from it.

Another popular line in the hotel business at that time was to "benchmark" other companies. That translates to "we want to compete but not shake up the status quo." That is as contrary to entrepreneurship as any business model I have ever heard. Great entrepreneurs don't use the past to create the future. The Wright Brothers didn't try to put wings on the automobile. "Why" and "why not" are mind expanding questions we can use at any time.

DISTINCTION:

Nothing much changes if we don't use our imagination to go beyond the status quo. What do you "imagivision" for your life?

The plan, the "how," will come along soon enough. If you stay with the vision, the right people and conditions will find you.

"You can't go back and change the beginning, but you can start where you are and change the ending."

— C.C Lewis quoted in MainPublic.org

Other People

Who's running my life?

Joy and fulfillment will elude us if we are only as good as we allow others to tell us we are.

In the book The Four Agreements, Don Miguel Ruiz writes: "Don't take anything personally. Nothing others do is because of you. What others say and do is a projection of their own reality their own dream. When you are immune to the opinions and actions of others, you won't be the victim of needless suffering."

Especially when we are younger, we spend an inordinate amount of time wondering what other people think of us. To be more precise, we lose time thinking about what we think they think about us.

When I was in college, I lived in a mountain town outside of Boulder, Colorado. One day I walked into the local bar and a man people called Milkman looked up from his beer, stared at my red patent leather knee high rainboots and said in some kind of mountain twang, "We don't do that 'round hea!" The judgement stopped me in my tracks. I wasn't accepted. I didn't fit in. I still remember it 30 years later. It took me a while to realize I didn't want to fit in. I didn't want to be Milkwoman.

Gaining approval from others has been drilled into us since infancy. Even as adults we tend to seek and therefore build a life around the "kind opinions" of other people.

Friends and family may mean well, or they may advise us in a manner that is self-serving. Either way, to sublimate our dreams is like slowly dying by one's own hand. Women are more prone to this as we are natural caregivers, but if you give your life away, there is no understudy for you. If you freely commit to give your life to another, make sure you love being there.

Who is anyone to tell you that you are not amazing with gifts only you possess. No one can live your life for you or know what is best for you. What others think isn't about you. They are in their own box with their own "mishegoss." (An expressive Yiddish word denoting craziness or senseless behavior).

Interpretation runs rampant when it comes to assessing what others think. When our boss frowns at us, maybe she just has indigestion. I once thought this guy was flirting with me in a gym. Actually, he was grimacing. Turns out his weights were just too heavy. If you are sensitive about your weight, and your friend says you look great in those jeans, do you immediately think you looked awful yesterday? It is our own self-talk that has us interpret the world the way we do. As Anais Nin so aptly put it, "We don't see things as they are. We see them as we are."

In personal relationships, give up any notion you can change or save anybody. It's not our job. If you don't like them for who they are, find someone you do like and can have fun with. Let them work it out. It is not our response-ability. Our "ability" to "respond" is to lift ourselves up and out. This is not mean. It is time saving.

Happiness is allowing others to be the way they are. They'll love you or they won't. It doesn't matter. Most of the time it is easier for people to project their stuff onto another to distract themselves from their own insecurities.

Love is not tennis. If one loses, we both lose. Lose the habit of taking score where you stand with other people. Great relationships are not 50/50. They are 100/100. 100% me and what I can bring to the table and 100% what you bring. If you only bring 75%, I still bring 100%. Don't give or take points away for not taking out the garbage or walking the dog. Just jump in with all your love and generosity. Give what you are best at. Dan likes to do the laundry. I don't. I light candles and burn incense. I am not sure he notices but it doesn't matter. I do it when I am alone as well.

I am thankful I don't take things personally. Here's why. When I showed Dan first blush of the book you hold in your hands, he said, "Who would want to read a book on happiness?" (Dan is more interested in performance and responsibility than happiness). While that directness is typical of the way Eights speak, I was stunned, then hysterical. I went back to the drawing board with a new perspective. I could have been mad, hurt, felt rejected, but those aren't the tools in my toolbox for living a joyous life. A happy life is lived in this moment and the next and the next. If you drop off the spectrum a bit, pick it up with the next breath. Who is anyone, and I mean anyone, to rain on your parade?

When we rebel against anything, it is because what someone is telling us to do is not aligned with our true nature. Children aren't born hating anyone or with prejudice. They are instructed how to view other people, races, and gender bias based on collective and cliched belief systems.

Go your own way. Be the light in your life. Be the light in theirs.

DISTINCTION:

What people think about us is none of our business. Most of what people say to us is not personal even though they may be talking about us or to us. Everyone has their own agenda. Misguidance and misinformation run rampant. Choose carefully.

Use everything to your advancement. Believe that everything is working out for you even if you can't see it now.

Learn to relax resistance when you feel it coming up. Maybe someone cuts you off on the freeway. Take a breath. Place your thumb and first two fingers together, squeeze and the tension will move there - anything to remind you that you don't have to live reactively. Resistance and anger slow down the life force.

Remember that we are spinning on a blue green planet at a rather rapid rate on an axis in the middle of billions of solar systems. When we lose sight of the improbable magnificence of being alive on such a planet our focus becomes narrow. So he didn't compliment you on your haircut. You're mad… really?

Most opinions are narrow unless they open you up to more joy or possibility.

"The question
isn't who is going
to let me, but who is
going to stop me?"

— Ayn Rand

The Tribal Bible

Belonging

People in tribes share common beliefs, follow a leader and have distinct ways of depicting their community. I was born into a Jewish family, but I am unfamiliar with the traditions and don't know any of the holidays. I prefer celebrating everything.

I don't choose to belong to a religious sect. I see myself as a New Yorker born again Californian living in a Colorado state of mind. Being from New York I possess specific tribal customs. Jaywalking in New York is a rite of passage. Here, I get a ticket. I am in the Grateful Dead tribe. My husband is in the Harvard Business School tribe. That's a whole other mindset.

If you love the collectives you are currently part of, be it fashion, spiritual, hobbies, or educational, and they serve you, congratulations. If not, or they were thrust upon you, go to what calls you.

Sports reveal remarkable talents, but I am not a fan, per se. I grew up at the ballet and not at the ballpark. Much of our identity comes from whom we align ourselves with. I am in Bronco country now. Most everyone dresses in orange and navy. It's a way of telling the world how strong they feel about their tribe. Same goes if you don Louis Vuitton purses or wear Patagonia and carabiners in a loop on your jeans.

We first learn our customs through our family and relevant institutions. Based on their collective belief systems, we acquire our initial view of other people, races, and gender bias. After that, the choices are ours. If you find yourself against someone, or another tribe, that is not happiness. That is a form of insecurity and resistance. Just let them be.

DISTINCTION:

The danger of being in a tribe first occurred to me at a very young age at sleepaway camp. I was friendly with all the girls in my bunk and then the camp director declared "Color War." We were all divided into different teams. What followed was enmity, competition, and exclusion. I just wanted my friends back.

The primary goals of tribalism call for adherence to certain rules. They honor traditions and exist to create meaning for their members. The payoff is belonging. The cost is believing our tribe is superior to all others in life… and death. To strive to be better than anyone is an elitist illusion of superiority. We all have our calling. Every one of us matters. Align yourself with the tribes that make you feel good and do good.

If you go back in time you'll find tribes that were essentially only concerned with their own tribal members. If you were a member of another tribe, you could be killed with impunity."

— Peter Singer

Conditions and Circumstances

Is my life a story I tell and retell?

Daily we find ourselves randomly bumping into conditions and circumstances aka obstacles. We make up some of them or use them as excuses. Others, such as weather and unforeseen events are thrust upon us. The trick is not to let them turn into reasons to be less joyful.

In the late 1980s Hilton Hotels transferred me to Atlanta. One month into the assignment, I was sexually attacked in my home with a knife in my neck. I can talk about it freely because even though it was the worst thing that ever happened to me, I refused to let it define me. But not at first.

Shortly after the incident, I attended a seminar of a personal growth movement I was involved with. The leader, John-Roger, was on stage taking questions. I stood up, told my story of woe, and added I had lost my joie de vivre and was afraid I'd never get it back. He asked, "So, Nanci, how do you feel now that you shared this with 300 people?" In that very moment, I realized I had taken on a victim mentality. I also knew I could release it just by my choosing. I had a relatively normal reaction to the event, but that didn't mean I had to let it destroy my life. I was in charge and I took charge.

I want to mention how my mother handled the news. A director from the hotel called her to inform her of the incident and that I would be coming home the following day. When I phoned home later that evening, the first thing she asked me was if I was alright. I answered that I was. She could have responded "My poor darling. I am so upset and sorry." Instead, she said "Then we are celebrating life." She did not make me a victim for one second. "Poor baby" has never helped anyone.

I have empathy for anyone who has had a terrible disease and has come through it. What I don't understand is why years later they still refer to themselves as survivors of the disease. It seems to me they are attaching themselves to a traumatic past event rather than acknowledging a free and clear present. To say we survived something sends the message we are still a victim of it. When we overcome something, it need not be our current identity. I had a cold last week, but when I describe myself to people I don't say I am a cold survivor. It's over. Ironically, the same people who call themselves a survivor of this or that have a greater appreciation of being joyfully alive. Best to attach to that.

On a lighter note, the last company I worked for bought everyone a Fitbit so we could get in our 10,000 steps a day and have a healthy competition. The problem was that the Fitbit only recorded forward motion, so swimming, yoga, burpees weren't counted. I heard people chastising themselves if they didn't reach their 10,000 steps per day. Who made up that 10,000 steps is a worthwhile goal anyway? If you are being held hostage by a piece of plastic on your wrist, throw your "fit'bitch" out!

I met a woman while on line at a farmers' market. She seemed lovely and was chatting me up while we were waiting to be served. Before she even told me her name she told me she had been trying for years to get away from an abusive husband. The story we repeat over and over becomes our identity. Good or bad, that becomes who we know ourselves to be.

DISTINCTION:

Counterintuitive as it may be, we are comfortable within our identity even if we don't like it. We fear change will bring on the unknown and upset the status quo. However familiar it may be, unhappiness is a nudge for us to wake up. Witness your conversations with yourself and others. Listen to your stories. They are a starting point. Instead of repeating our problems to friends, hairdressers, psychologists, parents, tell them what you are looking forward to. It's a new muscle to flex.

I once thought that if I didn't have drama going on, I would bore my friends. It turns out to be just the opposite. I speak the language of "Upliftment" and that is refreshing.

"Today is a new day. Don't let your history interfere with your destiny! Let today be the day you stop being a victim of your circumstances and start taking action towards the life you want. You have the power and the time to shape your life. Break free from the poisonous victim mentality and embrace the truth of your greatness.

You were not meant for a mundane or mediocre life!"

— Steve Maraboli

Becoming Un-reasonable (Without Reasons)

Are my reasons a cover up?

There is a line in the movie The Horse Whisperer that has stuck with me for years. The Horse Whisperer Tom Booker said, "Knowing is the easy part; saying it out loud is the hard part."

What stops us from stepping into our truths?

Reasons.

How many of us would like to reveal a truth about ourselves first to ourselves and then others, but give ourselves reasons not to? To fully step into who you are is to become free. To be you is to bestow the most magnanimous gift you can give to yourself and others. You are the most valuable currency there is. Anything less is akin to living buried alive.

Do you allow other people's opinions as a reason you can't be yourself? Why? Is any loss of inheritance or relationship worth it if you let them strip you of your dignity and only chance to be happy? Happiness and freedom go hand in hand.

DISTINCTION:

Any time you don't feel free to move in a direction of your choosing, examine your reasoning:

- You may have given your power to another person or institution.
- You may find yourself justifying staying safe.
- You spend time arguing for your limitations.
- Outside conditions seem insurmountable.
- Other people's opinions matter more than choosing what you know is right for you

What if you were to become unreasonable? In other words, you created the life you want despite so called reasons.

- I'll work out at a gym after I lose a few pounds.
- I'll take this job over the one I really want because it's close to home.
- I can't ask him out. He's too good looking.
- I'm in a wheelchair. How can I play sports?

Some reasons are valid. Some are a place to hide. Either way, the lives we live are born out of our reasons.

"Those who cannot change their minds cannot change anything."

— George Bernard Shaw

Incoming!

My point of power

Bombs Away! Here they come. And another and another and another. I'm talking about the deluge of thoughts that bombard us every day. Thought machines – all of us. Meditation and coma are the only two ways I know to possibly fend off the onslaught.

Are all these thoughts true? We have already revealed how our biases, perspective, perception, and memory have their way with us. We are like volcanos with our thoughts flowing as lava might – sloppy and everywhere. A hot mess much of the time.

Do your thoughts sound like constant chatter? Reliving the past, criticizing yourself and others, making promises you won't keep. Do they portend doom, fantasize about winning the lottery, regurgitate something someone said twenty years ago? Do you watch television or people in general and wonder how you measure up to this one or that one? Do those thoughts then turn into jealousy, fear, envy, superiority?

As I write this, I have had thoughts that range from hitting the New York Times Best Seller List to wondering if anyone but me will ever read these words. What has changed for me over time is

I now observe what enters my mind. In observation you become free. It's not *your* thought, necessarily. It's a thought. Maybe the news or the ad on the bus put it there. Follow it if it livens you up or pass on it altogether.

A century ago, science had yet to prove our thoughts had a powerful effect on our autonomic and immune systems, but now we know they are highly accountable for our entire state of well-being. Body, mind, and spirit are one integrated system. We can use our thoughts to start a war or usher in peace, wage happiness or experience distress.

When I speak with people about controlling the mind, some are curious how to stop the chatter. The chatter is never ending. It is the content we learn to switch on or off.

We are not our thoughts. Our minds are created to pick up cues and stimuli, but we don't have to entertain them all. Think of the right and left ears as doors in your head. Thoughts walk in through one ear, introduce themselves, and it is up to you whether you choose to serve them or not. If they disturb you, show them the door. Consciously turn your attention elsewhere. That is how you build a high form of self-awareness.

Eastern traditions teach us to become the observer of the ongoing chatter. If we can observe something, we cannot be it. To observe something is to stand apart from it, be separate. A fish doesn't observe it is in water. The fish and water are one. On the other hand, we have a rudder. We can steer clear of thoughts that disturb us. Think of things that nourish your life force, not deplete it.

"Think differently," said Einstein. What he is saying is have the kind of thoughts free from what's been thought before.

Imagine someone recorded your thoughts for an entire day. Mine would sound like, "What should I have for dinner, there is a stain on the couch, I should call Gail back, what will I wear today, I need a bikini wax, I wonder if I should get free range eggs, did David ever really like me, this song reminds me of summer, I'll put the garbage out, I'll write a book, it's too late in the day…" Blather….

Nobody captures this like Michael Singer in the book "The Untethered Soul." He compares the constant noise in our mind to a roommate we share space with. If we were to pull our mind out of our head and set it on the couch next to us and listen to the roommate for just one day, we would kick him out immediately.

Think in phrases that match what you do want, not what you don't want. Thoughts such as "I don't want to be lonely" emphasize "lonely. A better way to state it is "I want to be in a relationship I love." When you send your kid off on his two wheel bike for the first time, call out for him to "Balance" instead of "Don't fall" so the pictures in his mind translate to the outcome you do want, not what you don't want. Always use your words to focus on the bliss, not the blisters. Polluted language contaminates desired outcomes.

DISTINCTION:

We tend to choose what to watch on television more carefully than we choose what to think about. Be picky.

Become the observer of your thoughts. Watch them carefully. They are the predictor of your future.

“The only place where
your dream becomes
impossible is in
your own thinking.”

— Robert H Schuller

The Complaint Department

My choice, my swivel

When you work in the hotel business, you get your share of complaints. The objective is to handle them quickly in such a way that the guest feels happy and even grateful.

As mentioned earlier, inside every complaint is a request. Complaints are always about not having expectations met. The problem may be true, and some may be made up. It's not our job to argue. It is our sole purpose to make our guests completely pleased with the resolution. This has great application to how we treat ourselves in our everyday lives.

Complaints come in many disguises: disagreements, grievances, unsatisfactory conditions, grudges, there is something wrong with them or there is something wrong with me. All these complaints are requests for something better. They will keep up their barrage until we solve them one way or another. Complaining is stage a base level of consciousness. Nothing changes while we are enjoying and justifying the complaint. Shift into stage two. Solution mode:

I know what I don't want. I don't want____________.

What do I want?

What do I need to give up? (Reasons, being right, old identity)

What do I need to change or take on? (Honest conversation, education)

Let's say a couple checks into a hotel on the beach and didn't receive a room with a balcony overlooking the ocean. The hotel is sold out and their reservation did not confirm ocean view. They can spend days pouting or can change their viewpoint. The room is gorgeous. They love each other. How great it is to be on vacation. Perhaps they could negotiate a room change in a couple of days or change hotels. Focusing on the solution rather than the problem is the way of the Happy Warrior. And as the Chief Happiness Officer of my hotels, of course send champagne.

A good place to stand is "All is really well and there are a couple of things I'd like to improve." Get on those.

DISTINCTION:

If you are whining about your guest room and you find yourself in an earthquake you, your attention will shift immediately (as did the seismic plates). What occupied your mind a moment no longer matters. You changed your thought pattern.

Be your own "MIRTHQUAKE" in this lifetime. Choose joy again and again and the thrill and privilege of walking this planet. That view beats an ocean view any day. As always, your choice.

Very little is needed
to make a happy life; it
is all within yourself, in
your way of thinking.

— Marcus Aurelius

Waking Up

Just what this says

Upon being hired as the General Manager of Miraval, at the time the number one personal growth resort in North America, I was taken into the bookstore by one of the owners. Out of all the self-help and spiritual books on the shelves, he pointed out "Awareness" by Anthony De Mello and told me if I were to only read one more book in my life, this was it. Friar De Mello was an Indian Jesuit priest and psychotherapist.

In "Awareness," the author suggests we walk around asleep to our true nature. We marry asleep, parent asleep, and don't experience the joy of being fully awake. What he means is we don't realize we are autonomous with the ability to act independently of societal, cultural, and religious pressure to be a certain way.

He goes on to say that when we allow outside conditions and people's opinions to inform and conform us, we are puppets. When we were in high school, we were all very much asleep to our true nature. What mattered was being the most popular, getting into the right college, most rebellious. We were pretty much asleep to choosing outside of the constructed options. Facebook continues our high school experience. It's one thing to share puppy pictures and find an old classmate. We are still asleep if we are comparing ourselves to others, wistful at their pretenses, and posting our own. When we identify ourselves with a profession, wealth, or anything else, it is a slippery slope, and so will happiness be. Someone is always going to come along who is brighter, younger, and more connected.

DISTINCTION:

Learn to distinguish the voices in your head. Are you still living in Kansas even though you dream of living by the beach and surfing every day? If you are not where or who you want to be, find out who is masquerading as you. Thank them for meaning well, then leave your baggage behind as you trade their life for your own.

"Happiness is our natural state. It is the natural state of little children, to whom the kingdom belongs until they have been polluted by the stupidity of society and culture. To acquire happiness, you don't have to do anything, because happiness cannot be acquired. Does anybody know why? Because we have it already. How can you acquire what you already have? Then why don't you experience it? Because you've got to drop something. You've got to drop illusions. You don't have to add anything in order to be happy; you've got to drop something. Life is easy, life is delightful. It's only hard on your illusions, your ambitions, your greed, your cravings. Do you know where these things come from? From having identified with all kinds of labels!"

— Anthony De Mello, Awareness

Midlife Crisis at Thirty

A nudge from your higher self

I recall the day I turned thirty because I got scared. Scared that my identity was in jeopardy. I was sure that life as I knew it was over. It really felt like a crisis to me. Who was I if I wasn't "Tall and tan and young and lovely?" That had been my theme song for so long. (Except that I am 5'2")!

We are designed to bump into ourselves now and again and it usually occurs when we are in some type of crisis. Think of it as a nudge from your inner being telling you to take a good look at the state of your union – mind, body, and spirit. Are all parts thriving? Is your mind happy? Is your body strong to be your carriage? Do you sense your place in the universe? I wonder if the person who made up the term "midlife crisis" actually meant "midwife crisis." In other words, time to usher in something new and of great value into the world. This could its calling card.

No matter what you think is the meaning of life, if you feel good, there will be no midlife crisis at any age. Happiness is the great eraser.

DISTINCTION:

You will never be as young again as you are right now. These are the good old days.

"I think midlife is when the universe gently places her hands upon your shoulders, pulls you close, and whispers in your ear: I'm not screwing around. It's time. All of this pretending and performing – these coping mechanisms that you've developed to protect yourself from feeling inadequate and getting hurt – has to go. Your armor is preventing you from growing into your gifts. I understand that you needed these protections when you were small. I understand that you believed your armor could help you secure all of the things you needed to feel worthy of love and belonging, but you're still searching and you're more lost than ever.

Time is growing short. There are unexplored adventures ahead of you. You can't live the rest of your life worried about what other people think. You were born worthy of love and belonging. Courage and daring are coursing through you. You were made to live and love with your whole heart. It's time to show up and be seen."

— Brené Brown,
Blog, May 2018

We all Have Big "Buts"

What stops me?

You may have noticed that when people use the word "but" in a sentence what follows the "but" is the true gist of their communication rendering the first part meaningless.

"I want to marry you, but I love someone else."

"I would take the job, but I don't want to live in the south."

Anything before "but" is hokum. So if someone states, "I am happy to pick up the groceries after work, but the store may be closed if I decide to go to the gym first," it is advisable to pick up your own ice cream. Their "but" is too big.

DISTINCTION:

Unless examined carefully, the language we use gives us the lives we have. Our dreams and destiny are the results of our words. Notice if your big "but" is in the way of what you want in life. It could originate from a neural rut or one of the other voices you've invited in having its way with you. Examine it for what it is. If it's not in line with your dreams, just tell it to "'but' out."

We Live in a Semantic Universe

The power of language

Life is a conversation we have first with ourselves either in our head or out loud, and then with others. Then there are those of us who don't know what we think until we speak. You know who you are! I raised my hand.

Semantics is the *study of meaning* as it is expressed through language. We choose certain words and phrases to the exclusion of others to get our meaning across. For instance, "destination" and "last stop" technically mean the same thing on some occasions but mean other things as well. Advertisers, authors, and politicians are adept at using semantics to influence an audience.

During a hotel orientation for new hires, I would ask them, "What business do you think we're in?" The typical answers include hospitality, guest rooms, food and beverage.

I answer, "Those are just the vehicles by which we deliver happiness. We are in the happiness business." There is a language to luxury service. It can be summed up in the word 'upliftment.'" The concept of upliftment vs. mere transaction is to bring connection into it, a breath of fresh air and gratification.

We were always first in our market because we addressed the emotional role happiness plays in every interaction. This is true for any business. When someone asked a question, we wouldn't answer with "No worries" or "No problem." We would say things like, "Of course. My pleasure. Absolutely." The words we choose can lift someone up or leave them flat. Why imply effort and negativity when the objective is to please someone?

I ran a very hip hotel in San Francisco. My telephone operator was a grumpy methadone addict with eyes tattooed on the back of his head and a politically incorrect drawing on the top of his skull. To look at him was to want to cross the street. Yet, when he answered the phone, people knew they were calling someplace special. He delighted everyone with his wonderful greeting. I had someone once tell me when they were in a lousy mood they called our hotel to be cheered up.

Words have unbelievable power. The ones we choose and how we use them affect our well-being, and impact how others respond to us. Think of the "c- word." That is one of the few words that most interpret to be vile when yelled at someone. It's because its vibration is low and dense. If you yelled at someone, "You are a vagina," that has a higher vibration, don't you think? (Somewhat kidding here).

When someone asks, "How are you?" people typically respond, "Not bad, Fine. OK. Could be worse." That half-hearted response is a message they send to themselves as well. Why include the word bad? What would happen if they answered, "Great! Fantastic."

Positive cellular changes in the nervous system, that's what. A boost in confidence. It may feel pretentious at first to elevate your vocabulary, but it will become rote after a while with lasting benefits. We tend to be lazy with language as if it didn't have the power to transform.

I had a great valet team at my last hotel. When we discussed using uplifting language, they had fun with it. One of them told me when a friend asked him if he'd like some gum, he replied, "Absolutely, my good friend. Of course. The pleasure would be mine." Shock your friends out of mediocrity.

I have a dear friend of forty years who responds to everything with the word "interesting" and you never know what she is really thinking.

"I love swimming naked." Interesting.

"We got engaged after one week." Interesting.

I called her in the hospital after a bypass surgery and asked her how she was feeling. Sure enough, she said it was an interesting experience. Really? Not scary? Not vulnerable? Not hopeful? Not grateful? Her language was innocuous, but her tears betrayed her. How we use language can distance or put us in touch with our authentic self. Only from acknowledging we are at point X can we reach for point Y.

What message do you think gets sent to the body when we term our disease "My depression" or "My problem." When we personalize conditions, we tend to internalize them as a body part and keep them around.

I have experienced bouts of anxiety in my life. I could tell people that I "suffer" from anxiety. I prefer to say, "Sometimes I get nervous anticipating what might happen next, but I still go for it." Excitement and anxiety create similar effects in the body. How we interpret them shapes our outcome. We can run from the anxiety by calling it such or use the term "excitement" to boost our performance. One of the great golfers Tiger Woods once said, "The day I'm not nervous is the day I quit." It's a rut changer.

Listen to people speak. We use clichés that can be misleading and idioms that don't make much sense. I was once in charge of a conference for the National Earth Science Teachers Association. The keynote speaker opened the morning session asking, "Did you see the sun set last night?"

Many responded "Yes. Beautiful."

That's ironic. Any scientist will tell you the sun doesn't rise or set. The earth turns. Yet, we don't see a lot of advertising for "Earthturning" cocktail cruises setting sail at 7 PM.

As we continue to invent and make discoveries of any kind, we require new language to describe it. Albert Einstein had to make up "relativity" to refer to his discovery. Until the experiment in 1964 revealed a new chapter in subatomic particles, the word "quark" didn't exist. I bring to you "living happyliciously ever after. "

Concepts of time, past, present and future are human constructs. This is probably why when you leave the house, whether you come back five minutes later or in a week, your dog doesn't know the difference. He's just happy to see you. Similarly, when we entertain a memory of something terribly sad or horrible, that thought is occurring in the present as well. Even though we observe our thought as a memory, our mood and chemistry is affected as if the event is happening all over again. All negative thinking, even thoughts that bubble up from the past occupies mental real estate that could otherwise be used toward creating something wonderful.

DISTINCTION:

Notice your self-talk. Choose words carefully for they shape the effect you have on yourself and the world. Alison Armstrong teaches a fantastic course called Understanding Men. Her objective is to transform the world through how men and women relate. (www.understandmen.com). She interviewed thousands of men to find out how they think. What became evident in her research is that men really want hear to from the women they love that they make them *happy* – that is the word men used over and over again. I learned from Alison that to receive a gift or a great gesture from a man, saying "Thank you. That makes me so happy" puffs up his chest. It is different from "Thank you. It's great" or "I love it." I have practiced that. Sounds funny, but it really works. Semantics.

"A sizable body of research exploring the nature of consciousness, carried on for more than thirty years in prestigious scientific institutions around the world, shows that thoughts are capable of affecting everything from the simplest machines to the most complex living beings. This evidence suggests that human thoughts and intentions are an actual physical "something" with astonishing power to change our world. Every thought we have is tangible energy with the power to transform. A thought is not only a thing; a thought is a thing that influences other things."

— The Intention Experiment:
Using Your Thoughts to Change
Your Life and the World
by Lynne McTaggart

Your Solar Plexus is Not in Outer Space

Where does my truth lie?

While the term has a cosmic ring to it, our solar plexus lies not in space but at the pit of our stomach as a complex of ganglia and radiating nerves. Our gut feelings about things are felt there. I am sure you have experienced the sensation of butterflies or queasiness in your stomach when you are nervous. The gut and brain are in constant communication with each other sending signals concerning stress levels, digestion, and mood. Each system informs the other of a stressor such as public speaking or digesting a fatty meal.

Think of your gut as your personal oracle. Let's say you have a big decision to make. A company you admire extends a job offer to you. The caveat is you would have to move 3,000 miles from home. Whenever you find yourself unsure of what to do, try this: Close your eyes. Ask yourself, "How does my gut feel when I think about moving 3,000 miles away from my friends and family?" You will receive a kinesthetic response through your stomach area with one of two sensations. One may be a feeling of butterflies, expansion, and excitement. That's "gut speak" for "Go."

Or, you may experience a sense of dread, contraction, heaviness. That's "gut speak" for "no" or "not at this time." Maybe there are other things to consider before you take the leap. Chances are good the sensation will be a clear one. As clear as a book falling open to a page with an angel holding up a directional sign.

In an earlier section, I spoke of being attacked in my house in Atlanta a week after I moved in. One week before I made the decision to move into the ground floor apartment I had experienced fear in my stomach every time I thought about the move. I wanted to move here because someone I had a crush on had once lived in this very space (how juvenile) but my gut kept gnawing at me, "Don't do this." I called friends and asked if they ever had a scary feeling when choosing a place to live. They told me to take heed of those feelings. My gut clearly warned me not to, but I chose to ignore the message in spite of all the evidence I was experiencing in my mind and body. The day I moved in, there was a doorhanger on all the doors in the complex warning there had been personal attacks in the area. I still didn't trust my gut. I moved in. You know the rest.

DISTINCTION:

When you don't know what to do, ask your body. Allow the feeling in your solar plexus to overrule the mind in terms of clarity and messaging.

Here's another example of that. You can check this out for yourself right now. Stand in front of a large mirror with your hands raised in a Y wide and high above your head and say out loud five times:

"I am so depressed, I am so depressed, I am so depressed, I am so depressed, I am so depressed." Don't turn the page until you do that.

Regarding the mirror test in the last paragraph, I bet you laughed, or at least smiled, right? The mind can't hold two distinct thoughts at the same time. Body language trounces thoughts. The truth lies within the body and the body doesn't lie.

Thinking Effectively versus Thinking Positively

Let's get this done!

The most important choices we make in life is what our attitude will be in any given moment, no matter what the situation. That is the ultimate freedom we give ourselves.

Imagine walking into a shop you think is a candy store filled with goodies, but instead of finding chocolate, all the bins you reach into contain viewpoints. Pick up a clear bag, go over to any bin and design your life. I choose to put in my bag:

Freedom

Ease

Joy

Allowing

Aliveness

Courage

I choose them again and again every day. It's like setting your rudder to where you want to do.

On my journey to raise my happiness quotient, I came upon many who instructed me to think positively. I would take it one step further.

Putting a positive spin on things is not as effective as I had been led to believe. As Barry Pogorel said to me, "Nanci, I don't believe in positive thinking. The only person who needs to think positively is one who is thinking negatively. Otherwise, they would just be thinking." I like that. The so-called "putting lipstick on a pig" doesn't change the pig. If you create a positive affirmation and it is laced with doubt, can you state your desire in such a way that you believe it wholeheartedly?

Case in point: I recall preparing for a hotel owners' meeting following a month after we missed the budget by a lot. It happens, but I was plagued with worry about the outcome. Thinking "Everything will turn out all right" did not change the underlying fear that my boss would lose confidence in me and I might lose my job. Instead of just spinning the positive, I thought *effectively*. What caused this? What can we do to mitigate this in the future? How were we going to make up the shortfall? I could then affirm to myself, "I am prepared, knowledgeable, and the meeting will be a success." By effectively considering what would turn the concerns around, the meeting went well. The distinction is that I was sure I wanted a positive outcome, but namby pamby thinking wasn't going to get me there. See the outcome you want in your mind's eye and the right thoughts and actions will follow.

I have been a meditator most of my life. Important things occur to you when you still the mind, the noisemaker. I have a mantra that I silently chant as thoughts fight for their turf. My mind never becomes completely blank but clear enough to access a peace and clarity the active mind cannot. When the thoughts sneak back in, I gently replace them with the mantra.

You don't have to sit cross-legged with eyes closed to neutralize constant thinking. Create a sound or phrase you can use at any time. It is not possible to hold two different thoughts at the same time. To appreciate that is to understand the thinking process. Even thought thoughts fire rapidly, only one can be present in any given moment.

The mantra can be anything you like it to be. You can find one on the internet. You can also make one up. I like "All is well." Keep repeating it until you feel yourself softening and the mind will release its grip on any negativity. Mantras do indeed raise your vibration as well as moving your focal point off what you don't want.

In the Loving-Kindness mindfulness community, they recite this to cultivate love and compassion for ourselves and others.

May I be free from danger
May my mind be happy
May my body be peaceful
May I live with ease.

The beauty of this mantra is that it sends a kindhearted message without having attachment to specific outcomes. It's nice to send to people you love by substituting "I' with "you." (May you be free from, danger, may your body be peaceful, etc…) For extra credit, you can also send it to people who piss you off or people you are judging.

Alternatively, you could go for a run, call a friend (not to complain), or frolic in a daydream. And remember, we share the world with and penguins and toucans and soft summer breezes. It's easier to snap into another thought than you think.

DISTINCTION:

The goal with positive thinking is not to fool ourselves and be too "new- agey" about things. The goal is to focus on the best possible outcome that we know of, or better. When you desire a certain result, "This or better" is a great motto to repeat.

Do you recall the children's book The Little Engine That Could? The little caboose had a mission, but it didn't go up the mountain thinking, "I hope I can. I hope I can." Its mantra was "I know I can. I know I can."

"Once you replace negative thoughts with positive ones, you'll start having positive results."

— Willie Nelson

On Becoming a Genius

A mentality you can generate

Curiosity fosters creativity. Geniuses are curious about what might be.

We recognize someone as a genius when they shatter the status quo in science, the arts, or make a profound difference in the lives of others. We are at the starting point of genius mode every time we consider "What do I want in my life? What could be for those I love?"

Every problem seeks a solution. To be a genius is to be solution oriented. Once we recognize a concern, or cause for "worry," that is an invitation to spend time with ourselves and break out the genius juice. I recommend setting a calendar event once a week for fifteen minutes to think about solutions to what may be on your mind. It could be a problem or a wish.

Think of problems as your life force summoning you to new beginnings. A new chapter to be written.

DISTINCTION:

When we recognize something is amiss in our life, experience tells us that it won't stop badgering us until a solution is found. Problems stick around for a reason. They are our invitation to grow. To push concerns underground will not bury them. They are pesky and challenge us to use genius mentality.

More Freedom

Structures for more ease and focus

Something must be said about mind clutter. It's the "to-do's" in our lives that pop in and out of our minds bridling creativity and seizing the present moment.

I have never missed a deadline, or any promise made. I owe that to one special person.

Years ago, I attended a course that would change my life forever. David Allen, one of the world's leading productivity experts, and now a friend, caught me in my tracks with one phrase (paraphrasing) "We want you to have a mind like water." David explains: "This refers to a mental and emotional state in which your head is clear, able to create and respond freely, unencumbered with distractions and split focus."

We want to be able to control where our attention goes in any moment, not hijacked by to-do's. Important and unimportant ones are equally demanding our attention. Declutter. David's book "Getting Things Done" takes organization to a whole other simple and reliable level. Imagine becoming completely focused.

No longer will you be making love and thinking about getting the eggplant recipe from Shirley.

DISTINCTION:

Clutter is a source of dis-ease, distraction and worry. Create a system to capture the various agendas in your head. You will experience freedom to think clearly, creatively, and listen with full attention. Listening, with full attention, is a deep form of love.

SELF-ACTUALIZATION: THE WAY UP

The Seventh Sense

Don't underestimate the 'hu" in humor

The United States Military sanctions the notion that human beings have a sixth sense. Intuition.

I am going to up the ante. I think we have a seventh sense. Our sense of humor. It's difficult to think about living without any of our senses but could you imagine living a life devoid of amusement and laughter? The comedian Milton Berle refers to laughter as an "instant vacation."

The etymology of the word "humor" is curious. In Sanskrit, the word "Hu" means God. It is interesting to note the prefixes of the words Hu-man (godman) and Hu-mor (more god). Aside from opposable thumbs, what separates us from other animals is our ability to laugh (sorry, hyenas). When we laugh, we are completely in the moment.

I once tried to make Arnold Schwarzenneger laugh. Some of my colleagues refer to me as the Shermanator. Pretty much because I get things done. I had noticed Mr. Schwarzenneger enjoying breakfast at my hotel on several occasions. I never wanted to bother him but one day I went over to introduce myself. I said,

"Mr. Schwarzenegger, I am Nanci Sherman, the general manager. I want to extend a warm welcome to you. Please call upon me for anything. Also, you may be The Terminator, but I am known as the Shermanator."

He looked up at me with a very serious face and asked, "What did you do to deserve that title?" I said "It's all in fun. Nothing serious. The only thing I am serious about is how good our eggs benedict are," to which he replied, "Is it fattening?"

For sure, I will never be a stand-up comedian, or a sit down one for that matter. However, I still go get an "instant vacation" when I recall that interaction.

Humor was a huge part of my upbringing. My parents got married in Rodney Dangerfield's house. Rodney was a very a well-known comedian through the 1990's. Todie Fields and Buddy Hackett, also well known at the time, hung around a lot. I recall going to Europe on a class trip and Rodney came to the airport along with my parents. At one point, my dad left the group and when he returned he relayed that he had tipped the pilot. While we were all staring at him with incredulous expressions on our faces, Rodney said, "You've got it wrong, Dave, you tip God." I come from a world of one-liners. In that vein, I will leave you with the brilliance of Joan Rivers: "I'm no cook. When I want lemon on chicken, I spray it with Pledge."

DISTINCTION:

I once made a list about the characteristics I wanted in my partner. First on the list was a sense of humor. Laughter makes life easier. It erases pain in difficult situations. Fun and laughter bond people. Life is not only more meaningful when we can laugh with each other and at each other, it is truly a God send. With more Humor, you get more Hu.

I wish you a good belly laugh every day.

On Love

Toward "elationships"

I once heard Barry Pogorel define love. He said, "Love is allowing people to be who they are and allowing them to be who they're not." I had never heard anything so profound. Most of us think love is how people make us feel, and then we go about changing them so we feel even better which, to my knowledge, has never successfully worked.

Like someone or love someone just the way they are or set them free. No one can be our everything. Everyone sees the world just a little bit differently. If you need someone to be exactly like you, I recommend buying your mirror an engagement ring.

To love is to eat of the most bittersweet fruit. When we lose a person or animal we love we also witness the death of a part of ourselves. Conversely, our life is so much richer because of them whether they are still here or not.

Charlotte once told me that if I grieved heavily and for very long on her passing, she would have failed being a good mother and role model. She would not tolerate having passed without teaching me that life is joy.

DISTINCTION:

Love deeply. The scenery may change. People may come and go. Nothing is forever other than your ability to express love in your lifetime. You are the keeper of the flame.

Take that spark and run with it into the rest of your life.

"Shift" Happens

Taking back control

Sometimes our senses run senseless and something happens that changes everything. I remember clearly calling my mom in New York when I was at the University of Colorado upset over a break up. My mom let me go on and on until I said, "I'm so hurt. I can't take it!" My mom's response should go down in a Hall of Fame for all great teachers.

She listened to me closely. After my whining how depressed I was, she said "Nanci, don't be." I had an epiphany. That moment when you have instantaneous clarity. I could get over it by focusing on something else. Sometimes it will be something someone says, a line in a book, or you are just ready to hear it, and Voila! "Shift" happens.

Eventually, what you practice becomes second nature. One day you need the sheet music in front of you to play the piano, then seemingly out of nowhere you can play by memory. You go into a zone and rather than being the player you become the vehicle for the music to flow through. The same is true of happiness. One day, you awake distinct from your initial imprints, take hold of your rudder, and become happiness itself. It's like running through a field of flowers with no end in sight. Wherever you go, you are following your bliss.

DISTINCTION:

Charlotte's instruction, "Don't be" is a world apart from insensitive advice like "Move On. Get over it. Snap out of your pity party." To "move on" sounds like something you might read in an advice column. "Don't be," gave me my power back. I could continue with the depression or choose to elevate. Charlotte changed the way I would look at things forever.

People move on. You will too. Trust that everything is always working out for the best even if you can't see it right now. Do whatever it takes to remember that everything passes.

If you find yourself moping more than a weekend, ask yourself, "How long will I let myself feel like this?" A month? An hour? Let's see. It's 8:15 pm now. I'll mope for another 45 minutes unless I start to look at pictures of us. Then, I'll go until 10:30. That should do it." Get on with whatever makes you smile and don't play music that makes you cry. Action is the only way out of grief. If you insist on staying distressed, I have no judgement on that. Just know the choice is yours. Take some time and then "Don't be."

If there is a lesson in a break up, go for it. There is no value dwelling on what happened or whose fault it was. I don't believe in the pop psych term "closure." That's the ego trying to lick its wound. It is only interpretation after all, yours and theirs.

My friend Holly once said to me, "Whatever the question, the answer is love." I thought about that a bit, agreed, then replied, "Holly, whatever the question, the answer is airport!" I was half-joking, but she understood what I was saying.

My way of saying, "Next. Please."

"Letting go isn't about giving up. It's accepting that there are things that cannot be."

— Unknown

Different Strokes for Different Folks

What is the one true meaning of life?

I am not referring to deep tissue massage in this chapter. This is about what life means to you and me.

Stunning as it sounds, there is no meaning inherent in the physical universe. We make meaning up. What matters to you may not matter to me, and it doesn't mean either of us is wrong.

Charlotte (enneagram seven) and I love to banter and engage in fun conversation over dinner. When Charlotte eats with Dan (enneagram eight), he doesn't think it's worth speaking unless he has something important to say. They love each other immensely but suffer from a number of disconnects. Charlotte wants the meal to be enjoyable in every way. If there is silence, she feels compelled to fill the void with whatever comes to mind. Mom is used to talkative friends. "Small talk" bores Dan and he thinks it's rude if the phone rings and Charlotte picks it up. She doesn't see his "problem." At least it's someone to talk to! I get a kick out of watching and listening to their different viewpoints. Both are wondering what the other thinks the meaning of dinner is.

I have been to mindfulness retreats where nobody talks during mealtime. I get the premise. Be focused on one thing only. Chewing can be a meditation. For me, there was no joy in becoming one with the tofu. I'll pass on future retreats that require my being mute.

It's what we say about things that makes them meaningful or not. Not everyone wants to save the whales, be vegan or do volunteer work. Some find meaning in their career, their grandchildren, or proselytizing on behalf of some religion. All that matters is what matters to you. There is splendor and growth in diversity.

DISTINCTION:

It is up to us to generate meaning. Some find it through art, some climbing rocks. For others, it may be their children or pets.

Life doesn't end after the reproductive years, or an accident, or at retirement. We can always make up something new. What is important to us at earlier stages of life tends not to be as meaningful later.

If we say something matters, then it does. Create your own ceremonies, make the best sunny side up egg you have ever eaten, let two cars merge in front of you because kindness means something to you. Go to temple or church or don't without any judgment on yourself others. Make happiness your religion.

I don't believe people are
looking for the meaning of life
as much as they are looking for
the experience of being alive."

— Joseph Campbell

The Purpose of Life

My sole purpose

Joy and Freedom

DISTINCTION:

Channel your best self. Don't hand the remote control to you over to anyone.

Sometimes to be happy requires you be brave. To be brave is to follow your bliss, not the person lying next to you, or the critical parent in your head. You are here to experience your bliss, your power. your destiny.

"Whatsa Motto you?"

What do I stand for?

This is the vernacular you generally hear from a New Yorker when someone is asking what the matter with you might be. The "mattah" may be you don't have a motto.

My motto is "Living with joy."

It is my setpoint. It informs everything I do. When I am "off," I watch dogs in the park, fill my mind up with thoughts that delight me, any number of things that I enjoy. Even when things seem to be going south or not going according to my expectations I know without a doubt that everything is always working out for me even if I can't see it right now.

DISTINCTION:

Create a motto about what you care most about. Keep it general. It's like dental floss for the mind.

I am love, loveable, and loving.

Each day is a gift I shall not take for granted.

I give and receive abundance with ease.

I am free to be me.

I follow my bliss.

Where I am is great and the best is yet to come.

All is well.

Everything is just for now.

My Third Eye Needs Mascara

There is no formula, nothing to get "right" here

I was in a morning yoga class and the teacher asked us to close our eyes and gaze up at our third eye. All I could think of is my third eye must need mascara! I laughed out loud at how ludicrous and ironic this was. Here I am supposed to be uniting mind, body and spirit, and all I can think of is looking more attractive for a room full of people with their eyes closed.

We can stick to the stereotype and story line that people expect or throw in a few interesting twists. To be spiritual doesn't mean we are poor and don't have sex. Because I enjoy yoga doesn't mean I am vegan and wear purple. Because I love the Grateful Dead doesn't mean I ever dropped acid. (Or if I did, I'd pick it up for sure).

DISTINCTION:

Expect paradox and irony. That's pretty much all there is. When someone claims they are holier than thou, look behind the curtain. Nothing is tied up with a bow as neatly as people would like us to believe. Feel free to eat a kale salad and chase it with a shot of tequila. Should you feel judged in any way, fear not. It is the righteous keeping their sense of superiority in check. Check, please!

Monday, Tuesday, Namaste - The spirit in me recognizes the spirit in you, and I still want to look good. Mascara makes me happy. Do what makes you happy too.

"Once you label
me you negate me."

— Soren Kierkegaard

"Belief" It or Not

Do my beliefs stand in my way or support me?

What is the difference between make believe and make belief? When we make believe, we are fully aware that it is something we just made up. When we believe something to be "truth" we typically suspend further examination of it. In fact, the longer we hold a belief, the more we feel the need to defend it and keep digging our heels in. You could say beliefs hold us spellbound.

Belief and make believe all come from the identical place – our thoughts. Should we bump into a belief that has become an obstacle to our happiness, given the tenets of perception, interpretation, and perspective, we know we have the tools to alter the belief and turn the boulder in front of us to a mere pebble.

As children, we wholeheartedly believe in Santa Claus. ""Mommy and Daddy don't lie." Then we find out that what they told us was rubbish. Then later in life we make-believe to make it magical and meaningful again and fall for every marketing campaign about it. There is nothing wrong with that. I bring it up to prove a point. It is easy to suspend belief.

DISTINCTION:

Whenever Dan uses salt, he throws some over his shoulder. He is superstitious in the sense that he is preventing certain consequences from occurring by getting salt on the kitchen floor. What if he went on a low salt diet? Would his luck change? The thing is, pressed for evidence, he may admit it's irrational but better safe than sorry. It's a superstition, not a belief.

Even though many buildings are built without a thirteenth floor, if you are living on the fourteenth floor, guess what? You occupy the thirteenth floor even if the number on the elevator button isn't there.

Superstition is a cultural story we preserve and extend to future generations. via myths. There is no correlation to results or lack thereof by picking a four leaf clover or blessing someone after they sneeze, per se. Some create their own superstitions like wearing lucky underwear when they fly. If it makes you feel good, go for it.

In a world with so much diversity, belief requires faith, not necessarily evidence. If you insist that your bank account increases every time you throw salt over your shoulder, that's a belief. You could pour the whole shaker on the floor behind you and your balance will remain the same.

Me? I walk under ladders, but I "believe" that when I press my thumb and two fingers tightly together, good things happen to me. Flight upgrades, avoiding speeding tickets. What do you think? Superstition or belief?

Excerpted from American Gods by Neil Gaiman

I can believe things that are true and things that aren't true and I can believe things where nobody knows if they're true or not.

I can believe in Santa Claus and the Easter Bunny and the Beatles and Marilyn Monroe and Elvis and Mister Ed. Listen - I believe that people are perfectable, that knowledge is infinite, that the world is run by secret banking cartels and is visited by aliens on a regular basis, nice ones that look like wrinkled lemurs and bad ones who mutilate cattle and want our water and our women.

I believe that the future sucks and I believe that the future rocks and I believe that one day White Buffalo Woman is going to come back and kick everyone's ass.

I believe in a personal god who cares about me and worries and oversees everything I do. I believe in an impersonal god who set the universe in motion and went off to hang with her girlfriends and doesn't even know that I'm alive. I believe in an empty and godless universe of causal chaos, background noise, and sheer blind luck.

I believe that anyone who says sex is overrated just hasn't done it properly. I believe that anyone who claims to know what's going on will lie about the little things too.

I believe in absolute honesty and sensible social lies. I believe in a woman's right to choose, a baby's right to live, that while all human life is sacred there's nothing wrong with the death penalty if you can trust the legal system implicitly, and that no one but a moron would ever trust the legal system.

I believe that life is a game, that life is a cruel joke, and that life is what happens when you're alive and that you might as well lie back and enjoy it."

It's About Time

Allowing

Einstein was right. Time is relative, and not just in terms of the cosmos. It seems to speed up when we are enjoying something and slow down when we are merely tolerating it. It is also true that timing is everything. Just ask the person standing on line behind the person who later won the lottery.

One of the benefits to being happy is you find yourself in a state of alignment and flow. What seems like coincidence is a matching up of energies. Expect synchronicity. Expect things to work out. Expect the unexpected in the most positive way. Why not? You have no proof to the contrary. Tomorrow isn't here yet. While typing this book, I was on line looking up a recipe. As kismet would have it, the woman who posted the recipe I was looking for runs a book publishing company. Coincidence? Bring it on!

On a recent trip, a stranger at Newark Airport admired something I was wearing. At the end of my flight to Denver, I noticed she was sitting right behind me. While grabbing our carry-ons, we chatted a few minutes. I immediately liked Sonia. She had never been to Denver before, so I gave her my number. Before she left the city, we spent a couple of hours walking around and talking.

Almost instantly, a beautiful friendship was born between two writers and kindred spirits. The first question I asked Sonia was if she believed in coincidence or synchronicity? "Synchronicity of course," she answered. They are similar terms but synchronicity implies there is a greater intelligence at work. I have no doubt. We were both in similar stages of completing our manuscripts with talents to assist each other.

That brings me to what Dan and I made up years ago to describe impeccable timing. The word is *ROSROT*. It's an acronym for "Right on schedule, right on time." When your happiness muscle is buffed out, you will always arrive on time, get the best parking space, land the difficult tickets to the game, or find Sonia in an airport. Things are always working out as planned or getting better. We say ROSROT a lot

Things take time to form. People are busy. The thought, "Why haven't they called yet?" or "Where is the man of my dreams?" are expressions of doubt. Pouting and doubting only delay the process.. Change doubt to conviction. "Everything is always working out for me." "What do you have to lose?

In fact, when a cashier or taxi driver asks you how you are, answering "All is well" is a higher vibration and holds more power than "OK, Not bad."

This or something better will always come along. ROSROT.

DISTINCTION:

Timing is none of our business.

Maintaining an uplifted state of mind and being open to receive are cooperative components for designing your life. No prayer, affirmation, or juicing will make anything arrive quicker.

Trust yourself. If it doesn't work out, there is no loss. You can't lose what you never had. If every man I wanted to spend my life with asked me to marry him, I would have been divorced eight or nine times by now.

Plant your seeds and trust they will grow. Feel supported and you will be. Give love and you will be love. Be happy and you will get happy.

"According to Vedanta, there are only two symptoms of enlightenment, just two indications that a transformation is taking place within you toward a higher consciousness. The first symptom is that you stop worrying. Things don't bother you anymore. You become light-hearted and full of joy. The second symptom is that you encounter more and more meaningful coincidences in your life, more and more synchronicities. And this accelerates to the point where you actually experience the miraculous. (Quoted by Carol Lynn Pearson in Consider the Butterfly).

— Deepak Chopra, Synchrodestiny: Harnessing the Infinite Power of Coincidence to Create Miracles

Turn It On, and Turn it Up

Mediocrity is not synonymous with Happyocrity

Every person in your organization makes the difference between a good business and having clients / guests fall in love with you..

I had a very successful career as a luxury hotelier. It was important to me that our guests could "feel the love" whether it was the way their room was made up or how we interacted with them. I used a lot of role playing. While training a morning restaurant host one day, we role played my approaching the restaurant as a customer. The greeting she gave me was rote and lifeless. I then asked her to think of her favorite person in the world, someone she knew or didn't, musician, actor, or an inspirational figure, and we redid the role play. Voila! It was exactly as I hoped for. Use of guest name, feeling like the most important person in the room, articulate, enthusiastic, respectful. A glass of champagne on the house!

DISTINCTION:

To be outstanding, first you must stand out. Every interaction is an opportunity to show the world who you are and what you stand for.

When going about anything, call out your best self. Don't bring Mopey into the work place. This is your life. There is no work life, then real life. Your attitude is the key to your future. Make it a habit to turn it on, turn it up and watch a new kind of day unfold for you as well as everyone you touch. It's one thing to just "get through a shift." It's another to know you are the one that can bring joy to someone who may just think they are there for an egg.

What Kind of Person Are You?

You are, after all, humankind

If you are kind,
you will be happy.

If you are unkind,
you will suffer.

Golden Retriever Consciousness

A possible role model!

You could sum up the state of consciousness for this beautiful animal as:

Eat. Play. Love.

Now there's a life. Born blonde. Born to be mild. The breed has never won Best of Show at Westminster… and they don't care. Here today, Gone tomorrow. Happy.

Golden Retrievers, like all dogs and humans, like to have fun and see what they can get away with. Once, I was at the perfume counter at Saks Fifth Avenue with Smiley. As I was handing over my credit card to the salesperson and we engaged in conversation, Smiley snuck behind the counter, grabbed a sandwich from her purse, and tried to wolf it down before he jumped up, paws on counter, smiling as only a dog named Smiley could. It was funny. It cost me $10 to replace her sandwich but I can still picture the scene, and the laughter, and the joy of unscripted moments.

I had three Goldens – Smiley (the scene stealer), Noodle, and Buddha. We used to play together in the redwood and eucalyptus forests in the Oakland Hills of California. Sometimes during a hike, I would plop myself down to soak up the view and they would sit as close as they could to me looking out in the same direction. Tears of happiness would fill my eyes. If somebody walked by, they wouldn't say, "Wow, she looks surrounded by love and happiness." But that is what was going on. I was completely in the moment, no thoughts, just joy. I felt expansive, so happy to be alive and behold all the love and beauty my eyes could handle. You could say, I achieved the consciousness of a golden retriever – being in this world, not mired in the past, not fearing the future, but loving life now, now, now.

If all else fails, buy a Golden Retriever and name him Smiley!

Either way, I wish you daily joy and may you live "happy" ever after.

“Instructions for living a life. Pay attention. Be astonished. Tell about it.”

— Mary Oliver, Redbird

Happiness Check List

Are you willing to live a life you love every day?

What stopped you before?

How would you be feeling if you were living that way now?

What would be different?

Desires: What experiences would you like to have?
Obstacles: What "blisters" keep you from moving on?

Can you use "Follow Your Bliss" thinking to test if they are real?

Perception
Perspective
Interpretation
Beliefs
Other people
Genius thinking: What if?

Are you willing to accept anything less than your dreams?

Can you be brave?

What might your motto / mantra be?

"Come to the edge," he said.
"We can't, we're afraid!" they responded.
"Come to the edge," he said.
"We can't. We will fall!" they responded.
"Come to the edge," he said.
And so they came.
And he pushed them.
And they flew."

— Guillaume Apollinaire

Further Distinctions

Being happy doesn't mean everything is perfect.

Turn all your relationships into "elationships." Think in terms of upliftment in every interaction.

Your happiness makes a difference not only to yourself and those close to you but the world at large. Your happiness, therefore, is an unselfish act of service.

Happiness needs to be a priority. Before taking anything on, inquire into whether it will bring you joy. If not, can you find a way to be joyful doing it?

Show me someone who isn't happy. I'll show you someone who isn't free. To live happy is the ultimate freedom.

When you choose your thoughts, you project a new reality about to unfold.

Happiness is always just a thought away.

There is no day like today. Every day is a miracle.

To wonder is a great hobby.

I don't recommend hope as a strategy. Where would we be if we thought "I hope I don't buy a dozen doughnuts for breakfast today."

The only lesson we are here to learn is kindness, beginning with ourselves. It is why we are called humankind.

Feel the connectedness to all things. Even the acacia trees in South Africa give off a noxious gas in their leaves when herbivores like giraffes are feeding, and then they send a message to all the trees downwind to do the same.

Always have faith in yourself.

Self -doubt is you becoming your own victim. The payoff is you may not fail. The cost is you can't possibly succeed. When you find yourself playing the self-doubt game, stop yourself. Choose to be powerful. It's a thought exchange. Nothing more.

Everything passes.

Focus on your highest priority, then everything is simple. Choose what is aligned with living an inspired life.

Recycling is for garbage. If we keep dredging up the past, we face a polluted future.

Be mindful not to use others as an excuse not to feel good.

Never, ever give your power away

Because someone sends you a survey, you don't need to complete it.

Do you review your high school yearbook daily? Be mindful of social media.

If your actions are not inspired, do something else.

Don't listen to what people say. Watch what they do. If they hurt you, move away.

When in doubt, don't do.

Every decision regarding institutions such as business, politics, religion, healthcare, and even non-profits is ultimately based on their economic payoff. If you accept that, you'll be less pissed off at needing things to be fair.

There are many things to be mad at and think unjust. Get into action around them or think of something else. Journalism is essential to democracy but most news is fear based. When you feel your chest tightening, turn on some music and dance.

You find yourself in the Attitude Neighborhood of your mind. You reach the corner of Should and Could Streets and are not sure which way to go. Consult your compass to find where Bliss is located.

While dreaming of what you want, ask yourself why you want it. It will speed up the delivery. The "how" will follow shortly. Don't let not yet knowing how trip you up. It always comes to the party fashionably late.

What you focus on you get more of.

You are not in this world to live up to another's expectations.

Don't put off what you really want because you are afraid it may rattle your cage or the cage of another. Rattle away.

Sometimes to be happy requires you to be brave.

No one is responsible for your happiness.

Become difficult to offend. Remember, it's not personal.

There are seven billion people on this planet and seven billion different paths. No one knows what you are supposed to do but you. Be who you want to be and what you do won't even matter. It's how you think that is your purpose.

Conformity is a way to control people. Be aware.

Tuition is what we pay to get into school, "In-tuition" is where our real knowledge resides.

Chips shouldn't be on shoulders. They should be in cookies.

Become allergic to negative situations. Just move on.

I prefer to think of what I am for instead of what I am against." "Againstness" alone has never changed things. Ten thousand people against something doesn't have the power of one who takes a step toward what they stand for. Every war is "againstness" played out on a grand scale. I am reminded of Miep Gies, an army of one, who defied the Nazi occupiers and took in Anne Frank and seven other Jewish people during World War II. She was "for" something.

When you don't like the picture, change the channel or simply take out the trash.

All feelings are self-generated. Interpreted. No one can make you "feel this way."

To blame anyone or anything for your current circumstances is time well wasted.

To be happy is to be in love... with life... with yourself.

If we find ourselves whining about someone or something, we are the only one that can change the circumstance.

Living unfulfilled and unhappy is analogous to having a compromised immune system. Our susceptibility to illness increases. Alternatively, the stronger our happiness muscle the easier we can absorb shock and deflect dis-ease.

Your worthiness is unquestionable.

Happiness is upliftment. Unlike everything else, happiness is a multiple when divided.

Happiness and perfection are mutually exclusive.

Happiness is a good career move. You receive instant payment in gratification.

Create an event once a month in your calendar and ask: Is what I am doing and thinking working out for me?"

I have been blessed with a beautiful, healthy body and spend a good deal of time focusing on how thin my hair has become. What we focus on is what we have reduced ourselves to. Rather, create a love affair with all of you.

No matter who, no matter what
Your power is yours to own
You can achieve what you dare believe
Your power is your own
If a life you love be your true north
Think the thoughts that bring it forth.

— With love from me to you

Distinction Wrap-Up

We are all our own magic wand. We are either benevolent with ourselves and others, or deniers of what we really want, resistant to what we always hoped our lives and relationships might be. Below is a roundup of all the distinctions you require to follow your bliss and divert any risk of blisters.

Happiness is a gift you give yourself and others. To live joyfully is to feel love all around you even if you are the only one in the room.

One person's belief is another person's "huh?" Our ideologies form early in life. We innocently accept the imprints. As our belief structures take hold, it is often to the exclusion of exposure to alternate opinions. What I am about to suggest will and should shake your foundation.

Even though we treat our beliefs as true, they are in fact, firmly held opinions. Opinions are not necessarily based on facts and beliefs are not necessarily based on proof… and both are subject to change. The most important and relevant inquiry about your beliefs should be "Does this belief serve me or is it a block to my sense of well-being?"

We will begin undressing ourselves by examining the three biggies that are responsible for our current beliefs:

Perception

Interpretation

Perspective

Then we will glimpse into what we don't give thought to as that equally determines the quality of our lives.

Happiness is easy to measure. You feel great or you don't. What is on your mind either energizes or depletes you. \You could be lying on the couch talking to your friend about how bored and tired you are. You are sure of it because that is how you "feel." A minute later your partner comes in with keys to a new Porsche and says, "Let's take a spin in your new car." Tired no more as you leap across the room.

On occasion, life may appear to be on a steady course, but you can count on the status quo being disrupted and changing at any moment - with a phone call, a pair of keys dangling in front of you, or a newly discovered mindset.

Bodies tense up when sensing opposition. Understanding this is essential when it comes to relaxing our rigid structures. It is our individual perceptions of reality that are responsible for our point of view on everything. To think differently and reclaim control of our mind are at the helm of raising our happiness quotient.

We all have a bias on how we interpret the world around us – what we refer to as reality. We construct our viewpoint with partial information. The beginning of enlightenment is in realizing the variable nature of things.

Any strongly held belief about the way things are is a version of being born with blue glasses on. Even though we may complain, we are comfortable with the familiarity of our problems and attitudes. We defend them at all costs because to challenge them may imply we have to give a belief structure on which we have built our life and premises on.

Life demands we grow. When we become set in our ways, we contract a sort of rigor mortis of the brain. One day we may wake up to find we were running defense, but we were the only person on the court! Score: 0. No Overtime. To believe that happiness eludes us and favors others based on certain conditions and circumstances is a "chink in the cavern."

Being right is the booby prize. Do you really want to not have sex tonight because earlier in the day you argued over GPS directions with your spouse?

There is something to gain and something to be lost when needing to be right all the time. The ego may be tamed for a moment, but future communication suffers a setback. People who feel attacked tend to shut down and go inward.

Husband Dan has a chip on his shoulder about Apple. I am sure the tech world is divided on whether Steve Jobs was a genius or a tyrant. Who is right? Moreover, who cares? I could state how many Apple users there are and make him wrong. Instead, I move gently into the next moment and don't challenge his rant. To dispute him would be my needing to be right and making him wrong. It's his opinion. If I am up for a tug of war, there is a beach I can go to and play. Relationships collapse after so many years of ego tennis. Eventually, someone will serve someone with divorce papers. It just gets tiring.

Years ago, Mama Charlotte shared an anecdote with me. She said, "With the Krupp diamond, you get Mr. Krupp." She was referring to marrying a rich guy you really did not want to be married to, but you fall for the shiny object. It's an old saying but so true.

Whether you sell out for carrots or karats, know what you are getting into. Eventually, it will be your nemesis.

As they say, the writing is on the wall. Are we willing to look at it or ignore our feeling and predetermine to look away? When we sell out for anything inauthentic, happiness exits… stage left.

What we believe is nothing more than a product of thinking the same thoughts over and over. Those thoughts solidify into beliefs and become the foundation and structure on which we build our lives.

Conscious awakening begins when we can appreciate another perspective to be valid even if it is inconsistent with our own. This a wake-up call not to be missed. Judgement of ourselves or others causes stress and anxiety – the opposite of happiness. To consider other points of view as legitimate relaxes our uptight structures and makes us more easygoing. Perspective alters the notion of one absolute reality. Wobbly, isn't it?

Because we are the ones that adopt and create our beliefs we can change them. Beliefs are not a thing. They are a think. We are what we think. We live the lives we believe we deserve. If we are not living a life we love, it's time to consult our bus driver to visit someplace new.

"Good morning. This is your wake-up call. The sun will be shining all day and so will you. Don't pass on it. Pass it on."

Imagine yourself with no beliefs. What would you choose to believe in?

Interpretation is the architect of our lives. We translate our interpretations into our feelings and behaviors. The way we feel is *always* self-generated. Feelings don't exist outside of us. I was at a Tony Award winning show and the woman next to me took out her tissues and told me she expected to cry a lot. On several occasions, people were silently sobbing around me. I could see the protagonist's dilemma, but I wasn't near a tear. We are the interpreter, umpire and generator of all things we call "me."

Perhaps one night, you will sit with a glass of wine and wonder, "What did I interpret today?" The answer is "Everything." Then ask, "If I looked at things differently, how might I turn the situations that bother me to my advancement?"

Best not to argue with someone about what was said or what happened because unless it is on tape, in complete context, all our memories are fallible at best. Allow misunderstandings to be just that and start anew.

Soak up pleasure from the memories you love. If you dredge up a memory that feels like a black cloud hanging over you, it is. Release it before it drains your life force in the now.

Whatever we think about becomes our present point of attraction regardless if it occurred thirty years ago. If it feels good, take a "Blissbath" in it. If not, get out of the water. It is shark infested.

The enlightenment process begins when we become the observer of our habitual thought patterns. Once we begin to witness how our thoughts originate and why we think what we think, we can become objective about them and then modify and control them.

Understanding your enneagram type is a first step to real freedom. If your mind is the lockbox, this is the key. It is a stepping stone to leading to greater levels of peace, happiness, and consciousness.

To approach the enneagram is to travel a road inward. Understanding what motivates us and others offers us insight into to how people think and what is behind their behavior. That awareness vastly improves communication, solidifies teams and families, and calls forth much needed compassion toward others.

To recognize the value of the enneagram cannot be overstated.

I am going to let a secret out of the bag. There is a reason self-help books rarely work. Affirmations, how to books, have no ability to change imprinted patterns we are unaware of. We act out of our paradigm as if in a trance. We will continue to have the same arguments with our loved ones when we don't understand them or ourselves. That is why there are thousands of self-help books out there and few make a difference. We can't heal a wound we don't see. It is only when we can acknowledge what hinders us that we can move toward a more fulfilling future. The enneagram offers us greater clarity on all interpersonal dynamics.

Thinking, like breathing, is automatic but we do have the power to control both. When you find yourself in a situation that makes you uncomfortable, it is good to have priorities. Your happiness is such a priority.

To react is to fall back on predictable patterns. To act with choice in the moment is to be powerfully aware and conscious. When I was young and my mom would instruct me to pull my hair back off my face, I took offense and was really mad setting up a pattern to avoid criticism at all costs. Now I just embrace having a mom here.

Always keep in mind what you want as an outcome in any given situation. Did you really want to insult the representative at the boarding gate because the flight was delayed three hours. Did it help? Let your desires dictate your future rather than imaginary fear and threats to your ego.

There is an upside to complaining. When you recognize complaining it for what it is, something you don't want, you could see it as a seed for change. Inside every complaint is a request for a new desire to be fulfilled.

If I decide, "I don't want X anymore," that is a complaint. I could stop there and wallow in the complaint or ask myself, "What do I want?" "Oh, Y would be nice." Good. Now we are getting somewhere. The next question should be, "What is stopping me?" Let's say I come up with several obstacles such as, "I don't have enough money, I need a degree for that, my father will disapprove," consider the following:

For a million dollars, would that obstacle still prevent you from taking action?

What would you tell your best friend to do in the same situation?

Are you blaming anyone for your inability to move forward?

What do you need to have happen to move forward?

What is one baby step you can take?

We are only as limited as our beliefs and lack of imagination.

We need protection as a child. We need expansion as an adult. Life demands we grow and rewards us with a life we love and live out loud.

Happiness: If not now, when?

We are the defendant, judge and jury in our lives. We could live freely and unencumbered. It is up to us alone.

We attract to ourselves a tomorrow based on our consciousness today. Period. The future is predicated on the now. There is no pot at the end of the rainbow. The rainbow and the pot are one

The difference between "because" and being cause is use of imagination. When you imagine, you don't have reasons. You are creating out of nothing. Imagination has to do with the future, not the past. Use your imagination daily to consider what you want to have in your life.

Make choices from what you really, really want. If there is something you want and don't currently experience, look for the "real" or imagined obstacle. Crack it open like an egg. See what needs unscrambling. If the window won't open, try the door. If

opportunity doesn't knock, install a doorbell. If no one answers, walk on.

Nothing much changes if we don't use our imagination to go beyond the status quo. What do you "imagivision" for your life?

The plan, the "how," will come along soon enough. If you stay with the vision, the right people and conditions will find you.

What people think about us is none of our business. Most of what people say to us is not personal even though they may be talking about us or to us Everyone has their own agenda. Misguidance and misinformation run rampant. Choose carefully.

Use everything to your advancement. Believe that everything is working out for you even if you can't see it now.

Learn to relax resistance when you feel it coming up. Maybe someone cuts you off on the freeway. Take a breath. Place your thumb and first two fingers together, squeeze and the tension will move there - anything to remind you that you don't have to live reactively. Resistance and anger slow down the life force.

Remember that we are spinning on a blue green planet at a rather rapid rate on an axis in the middle of billions of solar systems. When we lose sight of the improbable magnificence of being alive on such a planet our focus becomes narrow. So he didn't compliment you on your haircut. You're mad… really?

Most opinions are narrow unless they open you up to more joy or possibility.

The danger of being in a tribe first occurred to me at a very young age at sleepaway camp. I was friendly with all the girls in my bunk and then the camp director declared "Color War." We were all divided into different teams. What followed was enmity, competition, and exclusion. I just wanted my friends back.

The primary goals of tribalism call for adherence to certain rules. They honor traditions and exist to create meaning for their members. The payoff is belonging. The cost is believing our tribe is superior to all others in life… and death. To strive to be better than anyone is an elitist illusion of superiority. We all have our calling. Every one of us matters. Align yourself with the tribes that make you feel good and do good.

Counterintuitive as it may be, we are comfortable within our identity even if we don't like it. We fear change will bring on the unknown and upset the status quo. However familiar it may be, unhappiness is a nudge for us to wake up. Witness your conversations with yourself and others. Listen to your stories. They are a starting point. Instead of repeating our problems to friends, hairdressers, psychologists, parents, tell them what you are looking forward to. It's a new muscle to flex.

I once thought that if I didn't have drama going on, I would bore my friends. It turns out to be just the opposite. I speak the language of "Upliftment" and that is refreshing.

Any time you don't feel free to move in a direction of your choosing, examine your reasoning:

- You may have given your power to another person or institution.
- You may find yourself justifying staying safe.
- You spend time arguing for your limitations.
- Outside conditions seem insurmountable.
- Other people's opinions matter more than choosing what you know is right for you.

What if you were to become unreasonable? In other words, you created the life you want despite so called reasons.

- I'll work out at a gym after I lose a few pounds.
- I'll take this job over the one I really want because it's close to home.
- I can't ask him out. He's too good looking.
- I'm in a wheelchair. How can I play sports?

Some reasons are valid. Some are a place to hide. Either way, the lives we live are born out of our reasons.

We tend to choose what to watch on television more carefully than we choose what to think about. Be picky.

Become the observer of your thoughts. Watch them carefully. They are the predictor of your future.

If you are whining about your guest room and you find yourself in an earthquake you, your attention will shift immediately (as did the seismic plates). What occupied your mind a moment no longer matters. You changed your thought pattern.

Be your own "MIRTHQUAKE" in this lifetime. Choose joy again and again and the thrill and privilege of walking this planet. That view beats an ocean view any day. As always, your choice.

Learn to distinguish the voices in your head. Are you still living in Kansas even though you dream of living by the beach and surfing every day? If you are not where or who you want to be, find out who is masquerading as you. Thank them for meaning well, then leave your baggage behind as you trade their life for your own.

You will never be as young again as you are right now. These are the good old days.

Unless examined carefully, the language we use gives us the lives we have. Our dreams and destiny are the results of our words. Notice if your big "but" is in the way of what you want in life. It could originate from a neural rut or one of the other voices you've invited in having its way with you. Examine it for what it is. If it's not in line with your dreams, just tell it to "'but' out."

Notice your self-talk. Choose words carefully for they shape the effect you have on yourself and the world. Alison Armstrong teaches a fantastic course called Understanding Men. Her objective is to transform the world through how men and women relate. (www.understandmen.com). She interviewed thousands of men to find out how they think. What became evident in her research is that men really want to hear from the women they love that they make them *happy* – that is the word men used over and over again. I learned from Alison that to receive a gift or a great gesture from a man, saying "Thank you. That makes me so happy" puffs up his chest. It is different from "Thank you. It's great" or "I love it." I have practiced that. Sounds funny, but it really works. Semantics.

The goal with positive thinking is not to fool ourselves and be too "new- agey" about things. The goal is to focus on the best possible outcome that we know of, or better. When you desire a certain result, "This or better" is a great motto to repeat.

Do you recall the children's book The Little Engine That Could? The little caboose had a mission, but it didn't go up the mountain thinking, "I hope I can. I hope I can." Its mantra was "I know I can. I know I can."

When we recognize something is amiss in our life, experience tells us that it won't stop badgering us until a solution is found. Problems stick around for a reason. They are our invitation to grow. To push concerns underground will not bury them. They are pesky and challenge us to use genius mentality.

Clutter is a source of dis-ease, distraction and worry. Create a system to capture the various agendas in your head. You will experience freedom to think clearly, creatively, and listen with full attention. Listening, with full attention, is a deep form of love.

I once made a list about the characteristics I wanted in my partner. First on the list was a sense of humor. Laughter makes life easier. It erases pain in difficult situations. Fun and laughter bond people.

Life is not only more meaningful when we can laugh with each other and at each other, it is truly a God send. With more Humor, you get more of Hu.

I wish you a good belly laugh every day.

Love deeply. The scenery may change. People may come and go. Nothing is forever other than your ability to express love in your lifetime. You are the keeper of the flame.

Take that spark and run with it into the rest of your life.

Charlotte's instruction, "Don't be" is a world apart from insensitive advice like "Move On. Get over it. Snap out of your pity party." To "move on" sounds like something you might read in an advice column. "Don't be," gave me my power back. I could continue with the depression or choose to elevate. Charlotte changed the way I would look at things forever.

People move on. You will too. Trust that everything is always working out for the best even if you can't see it right now. Do whatever it takes to remember that everything passes.

If you find yourself moping more than a weekend, ask yourself, "How long will I let myself feel like this?" A month? An hour? Let's see. It's 8:15 pm now. I'll mope for another 45 minutes unless

I start to look at pictures of us. Then, I'll go until 10:30. That should do it." Get on with whatever makes you smile and don't play music that makes you cry. If you insist on staying distressed, I have no judgement on that. Just know the choice is yours. Take some time and then "Don't be."

If there is a lesson in a break up, go for it. There is no value dwelling on what happened or whose fault it was. I don't believe in the pop psych term "closure." That's the ego trying to lick its wound. It is only interpretation after all, yours and theirs.

My friend Holly once said to me, "Whatever the question, the answer is love." I thought about that a bit, agreed, then replied, "Holly, whatever the question, the answer is airport!" I was half-joking, but she understood what I was saying.

My way of saying, "Next. Please."

It is up to us to generate meaning. Some find it through art, some climbing rocks. For others, it may be their children or pets.

Life doesn't end after the reproductive years, or an accident, or at retirement. We can always make up something new. What is important to us at earlier stages of life tends not to be as meaningful later.

If we say something matters, then it does. Create your own ceremonies, make the best sunny side up egg you have ever eaten, let two cars merge in front of you because kindness means something to you. Go to temple or church or don't without any judgment on yourself others. Make happiness your religion.

Channel your best self. Don't hand the remote control to you over to anyone.

Sometimes to be happy requires you be brave. To be brave is to follow your bliss, not the person lying next to you, or the critical parent in your head. You are here to experience your bliss, your power. your destiny.

Create a motto about what you care most about. Keep it general. It's like dental floss for the mind.

Expect paradox and irony. That's pretty much all there is. When someone claims they are holier than thou, look behind the curtain. Nothing is tied up with a bow as neatly as people would like us to believe. Feel free to eat a kale salad and chase it with a shot of tequila. Should you feel judged in any way, fear not. It is the righteous keeping their sense of superiority in check. Check, please!

Monday, Tuesday, Namaste - The spirit in me recognizes the spirit in you, and I still want to look good. Mascara makes me happy. Do what makes you happy too.

Timing is none of our business.

Maintaining an uplifted state of mind and being open to receive are cooperative components for designing your life. No prayer, affirmation, or juicing will make anything arrive quicker.

Trust yourself. If it doesn't work out, there is no loss. You can't lose what you never had. If every man I wanted to spend my life with asked me to marry him, I would have been divorced eight or nine times by now.

Plant your seeds and trust they will grow. Feel supported and you will be. Give love and you will be love. Be happy and you will get happy.

To be outstanding, first you must stand out. Every interaction is an opportunity to show the world who you are and what you stand for.

When going about anything, call out your best self. Don't bring Mopey into the work place. This is your life. There is no work life, then real life. Your attitude is the key to your future. Make it a habit to turn it on, turn it up and watch a new kind of day unfold for you as well as everyone you touch. It's one thing to just "get through a shift." It's another to know you are the one that can bring joy to someone who may just think they are there for an egg.

Follow Your Bliss, Not Your Blisters,
and you will never walk alone.

It is my singular wish that this book has made a difference in your life and you can see using it in a variety of circumstances, however important or unimportant. If you enjoyed the information, please let your friends know. I may be found on Amazon and on www.followyourbliss.today. I am also available for personal group and corporate discussion.

nanci@followyourbliss.today

Author's Biography

Nanci was raised in New York City and earned a B.S in Journalism and Communications at the University of Colorado, Boulder. The hotel business soon captured her interest and she caught theirs. As General Manager and Chief Happiness Officer for some of the most iconic hotels and resorts in the country, Nanci revolutionized the industry and consulted on leadership and motivation on three continents.

Nanci Sherman raises the bar on happiness. Her personal quest has been how to live an extraordinary life. Nanci studied with some of the greatest experts in the field of self-development / heightening awareness. She synthesized their teachings, expanded upon them, and translated this into her work success and life. You could say she is "terminally" happy and wants to pass that recipe for joy onto you. You will find her enthusiasm to be infectious, and her insights to be profound.

She is following her bliss, not her blisters, and is living "happy" ever after.

CPSIA information can be obtained
at www.ICGtesting.com
Printed in the USA
LVHW081408200820
663735LV00010B/203

9 781729 379608